GOD
AND HIS
ATTRIBUTES:

LESSONS ON ISLAMIC DOCTRINE

(BOOK ONE)

SAYYID MUJTABA MUSAVI LARI

TRANSLATED BY:
HAMID ALGAR

GOD

AND HIS
ATTRIBUTES:

LESSONS ON
ISLAMIC DOCTRINE

(BOOK ONE)

SAYYID MUJTABA MUSAVI LARI

TRANSLATED BY:
HAMID ALGAR

GOD
AND HIS
ATTRIBUTES:

LESSONS ON
ISLAMIC DOCTRINE
(BOOK ONE)

SAYYID MUJTABA MUSAVI LARI

TRANSLATED BY:
HAMID ALGAR

Jacket Design by: F. Farhang

May 2002

ISBN 1-871031-07-9

May 2002

Musavi Lari, Mujtaba, 1935 -
God and His Attributes: Lessons on Islamic
Doctrine (book one)/ Mujtaba Musavi Lari:
Translated by Hamid Algar.- [S.l: s.n], 2002.
206 p.
Cataloging based on CIP information.

1.God (Islam) - Proof. 2.Imamite Shiites -
Theology. I.Algar, Hamid,   1940 - , tr.
II.Title. III., Title: Lessons on Islamic Doctrine.
BP217.2.M84.04952   297.42
                               M7 8-27720

Contents

About the Author

Sayyid Mujtaba Musavi Lari is the son of the late Ayatullah Sayyid Ali Asghar Lari, one of the great religious scholars and social personalities of Iran. His grandfather was the late Ayatullah Hajj Sayyid Abd ul-Husayn Lari, who fought for freedom in the Constitutional Revolution. In the course of his lengthy struggles against the tyrannical government of the time, he attempted to establish an Islamic government and succeeded in doing so for a short time in Larestan.

Sayyid Mujtaba Musavi Lari was born in 1314/1935 in the city of Lar where he completed his primary education and his preliminary Islamic studies. In 1332/1953, he departed for Qum to continue his study of the Islamic sciences, studying under the professors and teachers of the religious institution, including the main authorities in jurisprudence (*maraji'*).

In 1341/1962, he became a collaborator of *Maktab-i-Islam*, a religious and scientific journal, writing a series of articles on Islamic ethics. These articles were later collected into a book published under the title *Ethical and Psychological Problems*. Nine editions of the Persian original of this book have been published, and it has also been translated into Arabic and, most recently, French.

In 1342/1963, he travelled to Germany for medical treatment, and returning to Iran after a stay of several months, he wrote a book called *The Face of Western Civilization*. The book includes a comparative discussion of Western and Islamic civilization, and in it, the author seeks to prove, by way of a comprehensive, reasoned, and exact comparison, the superiority of the comprehensive and multidimensional civilization of Islam to that of the West. This book has recently been reprinted for the seventh time. In 1349/1970, it was translated into English by a British Orientalist, F. G. Goulding, and it aroused much attention in Europe. Articles concerning the book appeared in several Western periodicals, and the BBC arranged an interview with the translator in which the reasons for translating the book and the reception accorded it in England were discussed. The English version of the book has up to now been printed three times in England, five times in Iran, and twice in America.

About three years after the publication of the English translation, Rudolf Singler, a German university professor, translated it into German, and the version he produced proved influential in Germany. One of the leaders of the Social Democratic Party informed the translator in a letter that the book had left a profound impression upon him, causing him to change his views of Islam, and that he would recommend the book to his friends. The German translation has now been reprinted three times.

The English and German versions of the book were reprinted by the Ministry of Islamic Guidance for wide distribution abroad through the Ministry of Foreign Affairs and the Islamic Students' Associations abroad.

At the same time as the first printing of the German translation was published, an Indian Muslim scholar by the name of Maulana Raushan Ali translated it into Urdu for distribution in India and Pakistan. This Urdu translation has now been reprinted five times.

Sayyid Mujtaba Musavi Lari has also written a pamphlet on *tauhid* (divine unity), which was translated in England and published several times in America.

In 1343/1964, he established a charitable organization in Lar with the purposes of propagating Islam, teaching Islam to rural youth, and helping the needy. This organization remained active until 1346/ 1967. Its main accomplishments were the dispatch of students of the religious sciences to the countryside to teach Islam to children and young people; providing thousands of school children with clothing, books and writing equipment; building a number of mosques, schools, and clinics in towns and villages; and the provision of miscellaneous services.

Sayyid Mujtaba Musavi Lari pursued his interest in Islamic ethics, writing new articles on the subject. In 1353/1974, a collection of these articles, revised and supplemented, appeared in book form under the title, *The Function of Ethics in Human Development*. This book has now been reprinted six times.

In 1357/1978, he travelled to America at the invitation of an Islamic organization in that country. He then went to England and

France and after returning to Iran began writing a series of articles on Islamic ideology for the magazine *Soroush*. These articles were later collected in a four-volume book on the fundamental beliefs of Islam (*tauhid*, divine justice, prophethood, imamate, and resurrection) under the title *The Foundations of Islamic Doctrine*.

This four-volume work has been translated into Arabic, some parts of it having already been printed three times. The English translation of the first volume of this work forms the present book; the remaining volumes will also be translated and published. Urdu, Hindi and French translations are also underway; two volumes of the French translation have already appeared.

In 1359/1980, Sayyid Mujtaba Musavi Lari established an organization in Qum called Office for the Diffusion of Islamic Culture Abroad. It dispatches free copies of his translated works to interested persons throughout the world. It has also undertaken the printing of a Quran for free distribution among Muslim individuals, institutions and religious schools in Africa.

Author's Preface to the First Persian Edition

An intellectual and ideological vacuum is increasingly drawing man away from the perception of reality toward a whirlpool of corruption. Today we witness many of man's creative energies being squandered as he closes his eyes to the rich and surging ocean of culture and thought that religion constitutes and as he permits his intellectual life to be slaughtered by the ideologies of the modern world.

Today various ideas are being presented to the thirsty and distraught generation of our day that derive from the hasty and defective notions of philosophers and scholars with limited horizons. These ideas pretend to answer the needs of the present generation, but they do not suggest any meaning or purpose for life.

The mono-dimensional mode of thought that underlies these ideas is not suitable nurture for the sensitive minds of our age, and is not even worthy of consideration in any environment where intellect and logic still retain a grip on existence.

There can be no doubt that the various inequalities, cruelties, torments and disorders that can be seen throughout history, arise from the contradictions that dominate the world and the life of man.

We believe that Islam and its ideology, based on *tauhid*, containing , as it does, an extensive series of profound philosophical and scientific analyses of the objective world and external reality and acquainting man with all the dimensions of his being, has the capacity to solve radically all contradictions and inconsistencies and to guide man in the direction of sustained creative action to assure his future.

Every belief system, although its principles may be universal and its bases eternal, needs to be presented anew to each generation in accordance with the circumstances of the age. Thinkers and guardians of spirituality, who are acquainted with the spirit of the time and conscious of the need for more research in fundamental concerns in order to confront the innovations brought about by modern philosophy and science, must, therefore, pay careful, serious and wide-ranging attention to these questions, drawing on the sources of Islam. They must present the truth as the broad and progressive spirit of Islam demands that it be presented, and acquaint the world with the intellectual principles of Islam.

The present work is an effort to present, in a concise and lively form, a survey of the creedal bases of Islam, combining philosophical reasoning with simplicity of wording. Since our aim has been to present a relatively concise work, we have refrained from quoting the opinions of various philosophers and scientists at length.

The first part of our work deals with the topics of divine unity and justice. We hope that it will be a contribution to making known the views of Islam on these fundamental questions.

Sayyid Mujtaba Musavi Lari
Qum, July 15, 1981 (Tir 24, 1360)

Lesson One
The Development of Beliefs
Through the Ages

Among the fundamental intellectual topics that concern human life, religious questions enjoy a particular importance. They have always been regarded, in fact, as the most basic concern for the well-being and destiny of man and have produced profound insights and extensive knowledge.

Scholars and researchers have undertaken wide-ranging and comprehensive studies on the origins and motives of man's religious concerns, pursuing their researches with a particular point of view and methodology that governs also their judgments and conclusions.

The truth of the matter is that since the earliest prehistoric times, faith and belief have always been part of the texture of human society; neither in the past nor in the present is it possible to find a society in which religious issues have not been raised. The Noble Quran refers in several verses to the historical fact that heaven-sent Prophets constantly appeared in past nations where, in addition to their beneficial spiritual influence, they also played a fundamental role in the creation of human civilization.

The study of the way in which human life has evolved and knowledge developed, together with the knowledge yielded by the most distant horizons of history, shows that man was attached to religious belief before he became fully aware of the methods of rational deduction.

The first era of man's knowledge and industry does not, therefore, enjoy primacy over the earliest eras of religion and belief. It may even be claimed that human endeavor in the realm of religion and belief has been more strenuous and longer-lasting than his efforts in the area of knowledge and art, for the knowledge of a transcendent reality that is the essence of the world of being is more difficult and less accessible than the essence of those things which knowledge and art strives constantly to attain.

The essential nature of the resplendent sun, which is the most manifest of all things, remained unknown to man for many centuries and its movements and effects were subject to all kinds of interpretations; although none could deny the luminosity of its rays, the minds of most men remained in deep darkness with respect to its knowledge.

The perception of great truths, is, then, impossible without logical examination, deduction and comprehensive study. If superstitions and religious myths are to be found among ancient peoples, constantly being infused into new moulds because of deficiency and weakness in thought and restriction in knowledge, this does not mean, then, that religion, with its doctrinal content, is false. Rather, it demonstrates the primacy and autonomy of religious aspiration in the very depths of the human soul and heart. Moreover, from the science that seeks to explore prehistoric times, we cannot expect that it will uncover more of ancient religions than the traces of myths and superstitions decipherable in the vestiges of primitive man and beneath the earth.

Since human conduct and activity are always accompanied by two clear characteristics—primacy and autonomy, on the one hand, and comprehensiveness and universality among the members of the species, on the other hand—it appears entirely logical that we should posit some origin for that conduct and activity in the depths of the human spirit. The existence of such a continuous phenomenon in an eternal and universal form, throughout history and prehistory, cannot be regarded as the effect of customs and habits; it is the manifestation of a primordial thirst and imperative instinct for truth. All religious beliefs, with their different aspects and forms, arise from a single gushing, abundant source—the primordial nature of man, which is neither externally imposed nor accidental.

First there comes into being within man's disposition, the capacity to accept belief, and then belief takes form. The same inward inclination that impels a person to intellectual investigation and research in order to perceive reality is an indication of man's need of religious knowledge. This, of course, does not mean that an inward state and predisposition is necessarily accompanied by a correct and fully formed belief.

In just the same way that the body desires nutritive substances without this desire, does not imply the goodness and wholesomeness of the food, the soul, too, seeks out its food—namely faith and belief— insistently seeking awareness of its lord and wishing to supplicate at His threshold. But the instinct that impels it to search is unable to recognize and assess beliefs and creeds, distinguishing the true from the false.

Scholars are agreed that religious beliefs have always been intertwined with human life. However, their opinions differ concerning the fundamental roots of religion and the factors that have played a primary role in its establishment and development. Their judgments, in this respect, are generally based on studies of superstitious religions and primitive beliefs, with the result that their conclusions are, in the final analysis, defective and illogical.

It is true that certain religions, lacking a connection with the principles of revelation, have been influenced in their appearance and growth by the social environment and similar factors. However, it is illogical to ascribe the foundation of all faiths and religious tendencies to material or economic circumstances and demands, to fear of the terrifying forces of nature, to ignorance or to considerations rejected by science.

Without doubt, one of the factors in the emergence of anti-religious ideas and a phalanx of deniers of God, has been the false teachings, the inadequacies and the intellectual perversions of the followers of some religions. The peculiarities and separate characteristics of each religion must, therefore, be individually examined when studying the reasons that have led men to adhere to that religion.

In many historical events, religion can be seen to have dominated all relationships. If religion were not a primary phenomenon, it would have to be enclosed within the four walls of material motives. However, what factor could have given religious personalities such firmness and steadfastness for the sake of their religious goals? Was it the expectation of material benefits and personal gains that made the bitter hardships of misfortune and difficulty sweet-tasting to their souls? On the contrary, we see that they sacrificed all their material resources prosperity and personal desires, to their religious sentiments and ideals, going so far as lovingly to sacrifice their souls.

In the story concerning the Pharaoh and his sorcerers, we read that he summoned all his magicians in order to defeat Moses, the one addressed by God (peace be upon our Prophet and him), hoping that with their ingenuity and magical powers, they might compel him to submit. But thanks to the miraculous power vested in Moses, they were overpowered and they turned to the true belief. The furious Pharaoh, whose arrogance had been broken, began to slander and threaten them, saying he would punish them with the worst of tortures: the severance of their limbs.   But a profound revolution had taken place in the souls of the sorcerers; they remained firm and steadfast in the face of the threats and cajoling of the Pharaoh and his painful tortures. They replied, with remarkable fortitude, *"..give orders for us to be tortured; your writ runs only in this narrow world."* (20:72).

This was a clear display of the strength of the innate desire for truth and reality in man when confronted with suppression, coercion and brute force. Men who had lived at the very heart of the Pharaoh's apparatus and had benefited from it, raised up their heads in rebellion and were ready to renounce their own lives.

The specific inclination of man to religious concerns cannot, therefore, be explained in terms of materialist interpretations; on the contrary, incidents such as that of the sorcerers demonstrate the primacy of the religious sense in man.

Illogical beliefs do not pertain only to religious questions. Before they were properly refined, many of the sciences were commingled with superstitions. Men found their way from incantation and magic to true and beneficial medicine and from unrealistic alchemy to realistic chemistry. No one can claim that if man once committed an error in searching for something, he is bound always to remain in error and will never find a way of reaching the truth. Those who believe in scientific philosophy and the primacy of the experimental method, accept that their experiments may yield erroneous results although they invariably give them the status of truth.

Those who deny God insist on the conclusion that God is the product of human thought. For example, the English philosopher,

Bertrand Russell, regards the fear of natural forces to have been the origin of religion. "In my opinion, religion is above all founded on fear: fear of the unknown, fear of death, fear of defeat, fear of the mysterious and the hidden. In addition, as already remarked, a sentiment comes into being enabling everyone to imagine that he has a supporter in all is problems and struggles."[1]

This is merely a claim, unsupported by any evidence.

Samuel King says, "The source of religion is shrouded in mystery. Among the countless theories of scholars on the subject, some appear to be more logical than others, but even the best of them is open to objection from the point of view of scientific proof. They cannot transcend the sphere of logical speculation. There is, therefore, intense disagreement among sociologists concerning the origins of religion."[2]

Nonetheless, we can respond that even if we accept the original and fundamental motive for man's belief in a creator to have been fear, this in no way proves that the existence of God is a mere fancy without reality.

If fear motivated man to seek a refuge and if in the course of that search he discovered a certain reality (God), is there any objection to be made? If fear is the cause for the discovery of a certain thing, can we say that that thing is imaginary and unreal because it was fear that prompted man to seek it out?

It would surely be illogical to maintain, for example, that the science of medicine has no reality because man has sought and discovered it out of fear, fear of disease and death? The truth of the matter is that the science of medicine is a reality, irrespective of whether the original motive of man in discovering it was fear of disease and death or some other factor.

In all the affairs and occurrences of life, belief in a wise and powerful Lord is a real refuge and strong support. This is quite a different matter from whether or not men's motive in searching it out was fear of vicissitudes and the search for a refuge or not. The two matters are quite separate and must be studied separately.

No doubt, in the primitive stages of his life, man was, indeed, prey to humiliating and painful terror when faced with awesome natural occurrences such as storms, earthquakes and diseases. A nightmare of fear cast its inauspicious shadow on all aspects of his life and his thoughts, and in the unceasing struggle he waged against impotence and fear, he sought a support where he might take refuge from his terrifying environment and find inner peace. Finally, through unrelenting effort, he conquered the nightmare of abjection and fear and attained a remarkable triumph.

The study of the different stages in the life of primitive man, and the discovery of evidence that fear prevailed in his thoughts, do not prove that fear and ignorance were the sole fundamental factor in man's inclination to religion. Such an assertion would be the result of seeing only one dimension of the matter. General conclusions can be drawn from historical research and studies only when the entirety of history, with all the different periods in the life of man, is investigated and researched, not one corner of his vast and variegated history.

The domination of human affairs by fear and abjection in specific and limited periods must not be made the basis for a general judgment concerning all eras. Would it not be a hasty judgment to say that all the religious ideas and sentiments of men, the inclination to the worship of God in all periods down to and including the present, have been caused simply by terror, by fear of the wrath of nature, of war and disease?

In actual fact, the most firmly convinced among men are by no means the weakest. Those who, in the course of time, have raised high the banner of religion have been the strongest and most steadfast of men. A person's faith is never increased in proportion to his weakness, and the leader of a people in matters of religious belief is not the foremost among them in weakness, abjectness and impotence.

Is the belief in religion of thousands of scholars and thinkers the product of fear on their part of storms, earthquakes and disease? Can their inclination to religion, the result of scholarly studies, of logic and rational proof, be attributed to their ignorance and lack of awareness of the natural causes of phenomena? What would be the answer of an intelligent person?

Moreover, it is not in order to attain some kind of peace that man turns to religion. Rather, it is after attaining belief and conviction that he begins to enjoy the fruits of religion—peace and tranquility.

In the opinion of divinely guided scholars, the world is a compendium of finely calculated causes and reasons, the precise system of the cosmos bearing witness to the existence of a source characterized by knowledge and power. The confused and incomprehensible brush strokes of a painting cannot be taken as the indication of a skilled artist, but precise strokes and designs with meaningful content are indeed evidence for the existence of a talented painter.

*****

There are also people who regard belief in a reality beyond nature as to be the product of economic factors. They make strenuous efforts to establish some connection between religion and economics. They claim that religion has always been in the service of imperialism and exploitation and that it was the invention of the ruling, exploiting class as a means for breaking the resistance of the exploited masses. Religion has been used, they claim, to stupefy the deprived toilers and to encourage them to accept their deprivation. There is no doubt that, like everything else in the world, religion can be misused. When diverted from its true aims, it becomes a tool in the hands of profiteers who wish to enslave the nations. However, this misuse of religion should not provide opportunists with a pretext for mercilessly attacking everything that bears the name of religion. A clear separation must be made between perverted religions concocted by imperialism to stupefy the masses, and authentic, constructive religions.

It is possible that in many human societies, unfavorable economic conditions, stagnation and backwardness may coexist with religious belief. But this coexistence does not necessitate any causal relationship; one cannot be presented as the cause of the other. Sometimes we see a society enjoying prosperity and flourishing economically that is deeply attached to religion, while another society that enjoys similarly favorable economic conditions is totally averse to religion. Similarly, in an environment of poverty and backwardness, the sun of religion may set, while in another such environment, the influence of religion may be at its zenith. The obvious lack of congruity between economic conditions and the prevalence or decline of religious influence is a clear proof of the fact that contemporaneity does not suffice to establish a causal relationship. Some special factor must obtain for the emergence or disappearance of one to be linked to the existence or non-existence of the other.

We can clearly observe this lack of congruity in two societies that are both under the oppressive domination of the exploiting class. In one of them, religion has totally left the scene, while in the other, its influence has expanded.

Objective realities show us, then, that man is drawn to religion in a variety of external circumstances. Wherever religion demonstrates its appeal, one must look for the fundamental inward motive in the specific nature of religion, not in economic circumstances. In addition, when we examine the aims of the heavenly religions, we reach the conclusion that the provision of prosperity and establishment of a just economic system based on religion have been one of the reasons for the sending of the Prophets. This, too, is one of the reasons why men have gravitated to religion and one of the benefits humanity has gained from religion.

Lesson Two
The Depths of Man's Being
Impel Him to Seek God

Outside the complex system of his body, man has vast and vital dimensions that are not in any way confined by his bodily mechanism. In order to discover those aspects and planes that are beyond the bodily structure and physical dimension of man, one must search out the inward and spiritual structures of man and perceive the broad horizons of his comprehensive nature, together with the delicate and refined manifestations of his feelings and instincts.

*****

A series of special modes of perception exist in man's being that are rooted in themselves, arise from the very stuff of man's nature, and do not owe their emergence to any external factor. Among these perceptions are the sense of commitment to trust, justice, veracity and honesty.

Before he enters the realm of science and knowledge with all its concerns, man is able to perceive certain truths by means of these innate perceptions. But after entering the sphere of science and philosophy and filling his brain with various proofs and deductions, he may forget his natural and innate perceptions or begin to doubt them. It is for this reason that when man moves beyond his innate nature to delineate a belief, differences begin to appear.

Inclination to religion and belief in God, draw, in their initial stages, on instinctive motives and innate perceptions, but then they develop and evolve with the help of ratiocination and reflection. The roots of innate feeling in the disposition of man are so deep and, at the same time, so clear and evident that if a person purges his mind and his spirit both of religious concepts and of antireligious thoughts and then looks at himself and at the world of being, he will clearly see that he is moving in a certain direction together with the whole caravan of being. Without any desire or will on his part, he begins his life at a certain point, and again without willing it, he advances toward another point, one which is unknown to him. The same reality can be observed in all natural creatures, operating in a precise and orderly way.

If a clear-sighted man, still in the state of nature, looks at the circumstances surrounding him, he will distinctly feel the existence of a great force that encompasses him and the whole world. In his own being, which is an extremely small part of the great world, he will see knowledge, power and will to exist, and he will ask himself how knowledge, power and will could not exist in the world as a whole. It is the finely calculated order and motion of the world that compels man to accept the existence of a universal intellect that, lying beyond the world of nature, nonetheless designs and commands it; unless this be accepted, the orderliness of the world cannot be explained. Anyone assessing his position in the world can perceive that there is a power which creates him, brings him here, inspires motion in him, and then removes him again, without his permission or assistance being sought for any of this.

The Commander of the Martyrs, Husayn b. Ali—may peace be upon both of them—said in his intimate supplications to the Creator, "How is it possible to deduce Your existence from a thing which depends upon You for its very being? Why do You not possess that manifestness that other-than-You possesses, so that it might make You evident? When were You ever hidden from the inward eye so that You might need proofs as a guide to You? When were You ever distant from us so that Your traces and signs might draw us nigh to You? Blind be the eye that does not see You watching over and guarding it!

"O God, You Who have manifested Yourself to us with Your splendor, how can You be hidden when You are manifest and evident? How can You be absent when with Your unceasing manifestation You watch over Your Servants?"[3]

Nowhere and at no time has a thing made without a maker been seen, nor a deed without a doer. The search for the link between cause and effect arises from an inward instinct in man; awareness of causality cannot be removed from anyone. Likewise, the religious feeling, the search for a Creator, can also not be removed from anyone. Even a child with no experience of the world, whenever he hears a sound or observes a motion, will instinctively turn his attention to the origin of the sound or the motion.

The foundations both of practical life and of knowledge rest upon the acceptance of a cause for every effect. The norm of causality is, in fact, an absolute one which admits of no exceptions. Geology, physics, chemistry, sociology, economics—in these and other sciences, research has the purpose of specifying the causes and factors that determine relationships. In short, it is clear that science and knowledge are nothing other than the search for causes; all progress and advancement in human affairs result from the investigations carried out by scholars into the causes of phenomena.

Were it to be possible for us to find in a single being or corner of the universe a sign of absolute self-origination or creativity, we would be justified in extending that one instance to the whole scheme of being.

Of course, it is not necessary that the law of causality should always manifest itself to us in familiar forms. The variety and multiplicity of causes is such that an investigator concerned with only one phenomenon might not be able to specify all the causes. However, in all the affairs of mankind, particular and general, past and future, in the circumstances of the individual or of society, not a single point can be found that is accidental. Not only is there a particular order inherent in the creation of each separate phenomenon; there is also observable in the relationship of every phenomenon with other phenomena, as well as the relationship of each phenomenon with the environment within which it exists, a subtle and finely calculated order. For example, in the cultivation of a tree, the laws of the heavens and the earth operate in perfect harmony with the structure of its roots and branches. There is also a relationship of animals with that tree insofar as they draw nourishment from it. How is it possible that accident should lie at the origin of such orderly relationships?

If a phenomenon were to take shape at a certain level in the structure of being, unconsciously and on the basis of chance, this would furnish an excellent groundwork for the disappearance and destruction of the world. For the slightest disruption in the balance of elements and the smallest disharmony in the radiant laws of the universe would be enough to make things lose their moorings and the heavenly bodies collide, resulting in a massive explosion and the destruction of the world.

If the origin of the world were based on accident, why are the theories even of the materialists based on the supposition of a plan, an ordering, an absence of chance? If the whole world is the result of chance and accident, what is it that did not emerge on the basis of chance? If an existent thing came into being not by virtue of chance, what are its distinguishing features and characteristics and can they be applied to the numerous and variegated phenomena of the universe?

Now since accident is opposed to order and harmony, it follows that whatever bears traces of planning, design and calculation should be disharmonious and discontinuous, because the concepts of planning, design and calculation are opposed to accident and chance.

To suppose that accident is the infrastructure of the universe and its governing principle does not rest on any logical proof or scientific evidence cannot be accepted as a definitive solution to the geometry of the structure of being.

When the experimental sciences demonstrate that the elements and natural factors cannot exert any independent influence and do not possess any creativity; when all of our experiences, our sensory feelings, and our rational deductions point to the conclusion that nothing occurs in nature without a reason and cause and that all phenomena are based on an established system and specific laws—when all of this is the case, it is surprising that some people turn their backs on scientific principles, primary deductions and propositions based on reflection, and deny the existence of the Creator.

Education and environmental factors are among the causes that either prevent man's innate perceptions from displaying themselves, or, on the contrary, reinforce them. Whatever displays itself from the source of instinct resembles in its orderliness the patterns of nature. Those who have been left free to follow the original course of their creation without being imprisoned by habit and whose inner nature has not been colored by words and expressions, are better able to hear the summons of their inner being and to distinguish good deeds from bad and true beliefs from false. Irreligion, which is, in fact, a turning away from original nature, is, therefore, rarely to be seen among such individuals. If someone tells them that the world has no indwelling order and that it is the offspring of chance, decking out his words in philosophical termi- nology, he will have no effect on such people, because they will reject his theories by virtue of their own original nature.

Those who are caught up in the webs of science may fall prey to doubt and confusion as a result of alluring terminology. The limited knowledge that inspires arrogance in man is like a piece of colored glass placed in front of the aperture of the intellect and the original nature; whoever possesses this knowledge sees the world tinged with the color of his learning and art. He imagines that the entirety of reality is what he sees through the narrow aperture of his senses and intellect that are a prey to color. Of course, we do not mean that man should refrain from developing his intellect in order to safeguard himself against illusion. However, he should not be limited by or take pride in his limited knowledge and art.

Most people, instead of making their learning and knowledge a ladder for the ascent of their intellect in order to raise themselves to a higher level, remain stationary and imprisoned within the four walls of concepts and terms.

Man's original nature, once it senses danger, rushes to his aid. When a person is pressed by hardship and overwhelming prob- lems, when material factors turn their back on him, when he has no access to any of the resources of life and is drowning like a straw in a maelstrom of vicissitudes and death is but one step away—then an inward motive guides him instinctively to a non-material source of support. He seeks aid from one whose power is superior to all powers, and he understands that it is that compassionate and all- powerful Being who can succor him with His extraordinary power and save him. Because of his perception, with all of his strength he seeks the aid of that most sacred being to save him from danger, and in the sanctum of his heart, he feels the power and strength of that being at work for his salvation.

Once someone asked Imam Sadiq, upon whom be peace, to guide him toward the Lord, saying that he had been confused by the words of the polemicists. The Imam asked, "Have you ever travelled by ship?"

He answered, "Yes."

The Imam: "Did it every happen that the ship sprang a leak and there was nobody to save you from drowning in the tempestuous waves of the ocean?"

— "Yes."

The Imam: "At that dangerous moment and in that state of despair, did you have the feeling that an infinite and almighty power might save you from your terrible fate?"

— "Yes, that's the way it was."

The Imam: "It is God Almighty Who is the source of reliance and toward Whom men look with hope when all doors are closed."[4]

Even rebellious and materialistic men of power who are oblivious to the eternal power of God when they enjoy dominion, change when they fall into the trap of defeat and destruction. They forget the denial of God that their environment and materialist schools of thought had inculcated in them and they wholeheartedly turn to the origin of all beings and the source of all strength.

History records numerous examples of such persons who fell victim to difficult and trying circumstances so that the dust of pollution was suddenly removed from their original natures and from the depths of their souls they turned toward the peerless Creator.

In addition to the inner resources that are innate in man's being and help him to discover reality so that free from all mental constructs and constraints he advances on the path of his original nature, the external factor of guidance and admonition is also necessary to show him the way and to reinforce his original nature. It is guidance that reforms rebellious qualities and protects the intellect and original nature from perversion and obedience to false gods.

The Prophets were sent to make men aware of the subtle perceptions of their original nature, to make their godly inclinations flow in their proper course, and to give wings to their lofty aspirations.

The Commander of the Believers, upon whom be peace, said, "God sent His Messengers among men so they might question them concerning their covenant with God, recall to them the forgotten bounties of God, speak to them by way of admonition, arouse in them hidden wisdom, and display to them the signs of

God's power."[5]

Such guidance and admonition do not in any way imply extinguishing the light of man's creative will or depriving him of his freedom and ability to think and to choose. It is, on the contrary, a kind of assistance to his positive inclinations and instincts enabling them to grow and develop. It is through guidance and admonition that men are freed of their bonds and enabled to profit from all the dimensions of their original nature and to flourish with all of their beings.

The Quran says, *"The Prophet removes all arduous rules and customs that men had placed on their necks like chains. So those who believe in him, respect him and aid him, who follow the light that has been revealed to him, they are, in truth, those who are saved in this world."* (7:157) *"O you who believe, respond and obey when God and the Messenger summon you to life-giving commands."* (8:24) *"O mankind, in truth an admonition has come to you from your Lord and a healing cure for the sicknesses of your soul."* (10:57)

The first people who accepted the summons of the Prophets were men of pure hearts and enlightened consciences. The ranks of their opponents consisted of those who relied on their illusory power and wealth or were filled with pride on account of their paltry knowledge and deficient, illusion-tainted intellects, in such a way that their groundless arrogance prevented their inner capacities and aspirations from flourishing.

A certain scholar has put it thus: "In spiritual matters, too, the law of supply and demand prevails. If the demand for religion did not exist in man's nature, the supply provided by the Prophets would be wasted. We see that the supply provided by the Prophets did find customers; their fertile, unclouded and authentic visions found numerous followers and supporters. This is proof that the demand for religion exists within man and his innermost consciousness."

In fact, the basic preaching of all the Prophets was a call to monotheism, not a proof of the existence of God. They negated the worthiness of idols, of the sun, the moon and the stars, to be worshipped, so that man's inner and natural thirst for worship should not be satisfied by recourse to external objects such as these and they might, instead, seek all their aims and values in a firm arc ascending to the true object of worship. Their hearts should be attached to infinite perfection, and with such a faith ever ascending, they should constantly advance toward the source of all values and virtues, finally reaching their aim.

All varieties of polytheism and irreligion—the primitive form that is idolatry and the advanced form that is materialism—are the result of turning away from innate nature.

The progress of knowledge concerning religious experience which is taking place all over the world has resulted in discoveries that permit certain important conclusions to be drawn.

Based on the considerable data collected by sociologists, archaeologists and anthropologists, the history of religions now analyzes the religious instinct, together with the institutions, beliefs, customs and the factors that shape society, in a new way that is largely at variance with the explanations previously given.

There is now a current of thought that is constantly winning new adherents from various schools of thought to the effect that the religious feeling is a primary, natural and stable component of the human spirit and that it is an innate means of perceiving the supra-rational.

In about 1920, a German philosopher by the name of Rudolf Otto was able to prove that parallel to the intellectual and ethical elements in man, there are also innate, supra-rational elements that constitute the religious feeling. Attributes concerning God such as power, greatness and transcendence have the purpose of emphasizing that sanctity cannot be reduced to any other concept. It is an independent category that cannot be derived from any other category and cannot be identified with any other concept, rational or otherwise.

One of the peculiarities of the present age is, in fact, the search for a fourth dimension in the world of nature called "time." Like the other dimensions, it must be intermingled with bodies, and, therefore, no body exists in the world free from the time which arises from motion and change.

It is likewise a characteristic of the age that the researches of scholars have led to the discovery of a "fourth dimension" of the human spirit—the religious feeling.[6a]

The other three dimensions or feelings consist of the sense of curiosity, the sense of virtue, and the sense of beauty. The religious sense, or the concept of the sacred, is the fourth dimension and the most basic of senses. Everyone has innately an attraction and inclination to what lies beyond nature, separately and independently from the other three senses. With the discovery of the religious sense, the three-dimensional prison of his spirit collapsed and it was proven that man's religious inclinations are autonomously rooted in his being. They showed themselves even in ages when men were living in forests and caves.

Despite the primacy, autonomy and effectiveness of the senses of curiosity, virtue and beauty and the role they played in the emergence of science, morality and art, it was the religious sense that prepared the ground for the activity of these three senses, helping them to advance on their path and to discover the secrets of the created world.

From the viewpoint of a believer, the world has been designed on the basis of laws and a precise, well-calculated plan. This belief in an ordaining, wise God stimulates the sense of curiosity to seek out and discover the laws and mysteries of nature that are based on a chain of cause and effect.

The role of the religious sense in the development and advancement of man's lofty qualities, in modifying his instincts and fructifying his sense of morality and virtue, is undeniable. Those who follow the dictates of religion regard it as one of their most important religious duties to control their instincts and to acquire outstanding, lofty attributes.

Religious thought has also been a factor throughout history in cultivating the aesthetic sense. Primitive men produced their most creative works of art in order to glorify their gods. The remarkable temples of China, the great pyramids of Egypt, the distinctive statues of Mexico, the refined and astounding architecture of the Islamic East—all these drew on the religious sense.

Psychologists believe that there is a connection between the crisis of maturity and the sudden emergence of religious feelings. In this period of life, even in persons who had previously been indifferent to religious matters, the religious sense takes on a special intensity.

There is no doubt that inward summons manifest themselves in such a way that no obstacle can block their path. However, certain factors such as contrary propaganda can decrease the growth and development of inward feeling and correct thought, although such negative influences cannot result in the complete uprooting of natural tendencies. If such hindrances are removed, sound instincts resume their activity and display themselves by means of their inward creative effort.

We know that more than half a century has passed since the communist revolution of the Soviet Union, but the roots of religion are still alive deep in the souls of many of the Soviet people. Despite all the efforts that have been made over this long period by the rulers to obliterate religion, they have been unable to remove the religious sense from the masses.

The existence of materialist ideas in the world does not, therefore, contradict the fact that belief in God is natural to man. If a certain school leaves the path of original nature, thereby making an exception of itself vis-a-vis other schools, both in the present world and in past times, this cannot be regarded as disproving the contention that belief in God is natural to man; exceptions exist in all spheres. What history shows is that the materialist school was founded in the sixth and seventh centuries before Christ.

Lesson Three
God and Empirical Logic

Without doubt, social circumstances, historical and educational factors, and the various forms of human labor cannot be without influence on the practical expression of man's inward inclinations and his spiritual and emotional characteristics. Although these various circumstances do not create any compulsion or necessity in man's choice of direction, they may bring into being a more suitable environment for a certain kind of choice, thus playing an important role in men's view of things. These circumstances may even sometimes display themselves in the guise of obstacles to man's freedom and ability to choose.

As a result of greater familiarity with scientific and empirical deduction, the human mind tends naturally to shy away somewhat from purely intellectual deduction, particularly if the matter under investigation is non-material and insensible.

In general, man's mental faculties acquire strength and skill in the area to which they are most applied: matters lying outside that area appear to him unreal or unauthentic, or, at best, secondary or tangential to the matter in which he specializes. Man, therefore, tends to judge everything in a particular way.

One of the most destructive and misleading factors in thoughts concerning God is to restrict one's thought to the logic of the empirical sciences and to fail to recognize the limits and boundaries of that logic. Since the specialists in the empirical sciences devote all their mental energy to the sensory sciences, they are alien to matters that lie beyond sense perception. This alienation, this distance from non-sensory matters, this extraordinary trust in the data yielded by the empirical sciences, reaches such a point that testing and experimentation form the whole mental structure and world view of such specialists. They regard experimentation as the only acceptable tool and means of cognition, as the sole criterion. They expect it to solve every problem. The function of the sciences is to explain the relationships between phenomena; their aim is to establish the connection between events, not between God and events. In the experimental sciences, man is not at all concerned with God. One should not expect to be able to perceive supra-sensory realities by means of sensory criteria, or to see God in a laboratory. The sciences cannot carry out a laboratory experiment on the existence of God and then reach the verdict that if a thing is not physically observable and it cannot be established by means of laboratory experiment and mathematical calculation, it, therefore, has no reality.

In fact, no experiment can be set up to determine whether a non-material being exists or not, because only that which can be negated by means of experiment can be proven by means of experiment. Science and metaphysics are two forms of knowledge which enjoy equal degrees of validity and authenticity. A meta-physical law neither arises from experimentation nor can it be negated by experimentation. Thousands of scientific experiments are designed to prove that all things are material; they will all fall short of their goal.

The empirical scientist has the right to say, "I have found such-and-such," or "I have not found such-and-such." He does not have the right to say, "Such-and-such a thing does not exist."

Laboratory methods, for all their complexity and advanced state of development, cannot find their way through the unknown, dark and expansive world of the elements that is the object of experimentation; they cannot understand all the realities hidden in the heart of the infinite atoms; and, they cannot even discover the true nature of matter.

The empirical method has been very useful in developing man's awareness of the precise order of creation, and, it may provide a clear and novel basis for belief in the Lord through its investigation of the order of creation, for it indicates the existence of a conscious and powerful Creator. However, the aim and purpose of scientists in their researches and investigations into questions of nature and the mysteries of the world is generally not to perceive the Creator of existence. In the course of its continuous development at the hands of researchers, science is constantly uncovering the mysteries of existence without the scientists emerging, by means of their science, from the narrow and restricted knowledge given them by the current stage of their researches. If they were to do so, they would realize the connectedness of phenomena and the subordination of all things to a given order, and, thus, attaining two additional stages of knowledge and insight. First, they would be able to correlate all their sensory, empirical data, and then they would be able to draw rational conclusions and make interpretations. Without admitting the existence of a wise Creator, it is impossible to interpret convincingly the totality of the varied data yielded by the different sciences and the connections existing among them.

Practically, however, the work and the method of scientific thought is to formulate principles and undertake research without reference to God, so that a system of thought from which God is absent becomes the axis on which scientific work turns, causing man to be alienated from whatever lies beyond the scope of that thought.

At the same time, man's practical life is inevitably connected with the sciences. The results yielded by empirical knowledge embrace all the material aspects of life, imprisoning man within their four impenetrable walls, and it is hardly possible to find any natural tool among the means of man's life. This necessarily increases man's trust in the sciences and affects his behavior, inducing in him a state of doubt and hesitation.

In addition, the beneficial nature of the phenomena investigated by empirical science is tangible and apparent to everyone, in sharp contrast to metaphysical questions. Similarly, the material phenomena investigated by empirical science are well-known, whereas the opposite is true in the case of metaphysics.

The presentation of religious questions in the incorrect method followed by the medieval church, combined with enmity to all manifestations of science, was the most important factor in making empirical science appear preferable to philosophical and metaphysical concerns. In short, science appeared to be opposed to religion, not parallel to it.

Once empirical logic succeeded in pouring all thoughts into its own mould, it colored men's outlook on the world to such a degree that they were convinced that it was the only basis for accepting the truth of a thing. They assigned it supreme authority and considered it impossible to prove the existence of anything imperceptible to the senses.

So the empirical scientist, who is unaware of the method of those who know God, accepts and regards as proper, in the course of his life, whatever is compatible with scientific logic and thought. He grants himself the right to deny whatever is incompatible with his scientific method. His method is absolute trust in the experiment and regarding it as the sole proof for the correctness of any deduction.

In such a situation, when the whole basis of religious thought is ignored, the scientist finds himself without any principles for interpreting those secondary religious questions which appear in the form of commands and prohibitions. Being totally accustomed to the language of science and dependent on formulae, he is utterly committed to his own method and imagines the binding, simple and straightforward commands of religion to be without content or value.

This manner of thought is faulty and incorrect. Although the sciences have complex and extraordinarily precise formulae, the comprehension of which requires profound and difficult study, those same formulae leave the realm of science once they enter our practical lives, distancing themselves from the technical language of the scientists. Were this not to be the case, they would be restricted to scientific and industrial centers, libraries and centers of research.

Everyone can make use of such facilities as the telephone and the radio. The same holds true of all scientific tools and instruments. For all their precision and complexity, a little specialized instruction will enable anyone to use them. The specialist and the expert do not pass on their mechanical, technical knowledge to the purchasers of the device; instead, they summarize in a few short sentences the result of the toils endured by the inventors.

It is, therefore, unfair and incompatible with scientific logic to attempt to force the commands of religion (which cannot be compressed into a scientific formula, being both simple and universal) into the mould of one's own incorrect prejudices and imaginings, and then pronounce them worthless and insignificant, while ignoring their decisive role and their profound effects in our life. Practical instructions bear their fruit when they are proclaimed in a generally comprehensible language and become tangible for everyone in individual and social life.

Furthermore, if it were supposed that the commands and instructions of religions should be determined by our cognition, understanding and taste, there would be no need for revelation and Prophets; we could construct our own religions.

Man often overlooks his weaknesses, preoccupied as he is with his strengths. The science worshipper of the contemporary world is so proud of his knowledge as a result of the progress that has been attained in the experimental sciences that he imagines himself to have conquered and triumphantly taken possession of the world of truth. But nobody has ever been able to claim that he has attained knowledge of all the mysteries of the universe and removed all the veils from the world of nature.

One must take a broader view of reality and realize how slight is one's own drop of knowledge when compared to the ocean of hidden mysteries that confronts us. In the wake of every scientific discovery, a further series of unknowns comes into view. Throughout the centuries that man has untiringly labored with all his resources to know the world as fully as possible, the only result of his exertions has been the discovery of a few among the many mysteries of the universe. Only a few short steps have been taken on this path, and there is a whole mass of unknowns clustered around human knowledge like a cloud.

One must, therefore, assess more realistically the cognitive scope of the sensory sciences and their proper area of activity and influence. All preconceptions that are like barriers on the path to truth must be discarded in favor of a correct analysis.

Without doubt, the empirical sciences can inform us only of the external aspects of phenomena; it is only matter and material phenomena that come within the scope of their study and are susceptible to laboratory experimentation. The method of the sciences in attaining their goal, while seeking to benefit from each slight increment in knowledge, is observation and experiment. Since the fundamental concern of the empirical sciences is the investigation of the external world, in order to be sure that a certain scientific theory is correct, we must compare it with the external world to test it. If the external world effectively verifies it, we accept it; if it does not, we do not accept it. So, considering the object and the method of the empirical sciences, we must ask whether metaphysical truths are subject to sensory test and experimentation? Does any empirical enquiry have the right to intervene in matters of faith and belief? Is any part of the experimental sciences concerned with God?

To discover the correctness or incorrectness of a matter in the empirical sciences, it is necessary to make use of change and of the elimination of given factors and circumstances. This method is not applicable to the eternal, immutable and supra-material divine existence.

Material knowledge is a lamp that can illumine certain unknown matters with its rays but it is not a lamp that can eliminate all darkness. For the knowledge of a system is dependent on comprehension of the whole in its totality and a form of cognition that can unite all partial insights in itself, resulting in a total vision. Now, to imprison human knowledge in the narrow, restrictive confines of the sensory sciences cannot bring man to a total vision, but only to an awareness of empirical phenomena combined with an unawareness of the inner dimension of being.

Whether we believe in God or not has, in fact, no connection with the empirical sciences, because since the object of their investigations is matter, the sciences that concern themselves with material phenomena do not have the right to express themselves affirmatively or negatively concerning any non-material subject. According to the belief of religious schools of thought, God is not a body. He cannot be perceived by the senses. He transcends time and place. He is a being Whose existence is not subject to temporal limitation and place cannot restrict him. He is, therefore, free of need and exalted in His essence above any kind of deficiency. He knows the inner as well as the outer aspect of the universe; the world lies open before Him. Finally, He possesses the highest degree of every perfection and is loftier than whatever concerning Him might come to man's mind. We cannot possibly know the ground of His essence, given the inadequacy of ourselves and of our powers, faculties and instruments of discernment.

For this reason, if you study all the books of empirical science, you will not find the slightest mention of an experiment concerning God or any judgment offered concerning God.

Even if we do regard sense perception as the only means for

discovering reality, we cannot prove, relying on sense perception, that nothing exists beyond the world of the senses. Such an assertion would, in itself, be non-empirical, resting on no sensory or empirical proof.

Even if the followers of a religious school of thought had no proofs for their claim, to conclude firmly and forcibly that non-being reigns beyond the sensory realm would be a non-scientific choice, based on imagination and speculation. Some people try to propagate this fantasy in the garb of science and to present their choice as having been dictated by scientific thought. In the final analysis, however, the denial involved in such an assertion is unworthy of science and philosophy, and even contradicts empirical logic.

In *The Elementary Principles of Philosophy*, Georges Pulitzer says, "To imagine a thing that does not occupy time and space and is immune to change and development is an impossibility."

It is plain that these words reflect a way of thought that does not know what it is searching for. If it knew what it was looking for, it would also understand how to look for it. Since the activity of this mode of thought revolves around nature and the sensory realm, it will naturally regard as impossible whatever lies beyond the scope of its activity and the existence of which cannot be proven by way of sensory experiment. It will regard belief in such an entity as contrary to the scientific mode of thought. However, scholars in the natural sciences are confronted with a whole mass of unknowns concerning this very earth and tangible, lifeless matter, even though they are constantly in touch with it (apart from which the material universe, with its countless mysteries and secrets, does not consist simply of this globe on which we live). Such scholars have, then, the right only to say, "Since the supernatural realm lies beyond the scope of my professional tools, I remain silent and cannot utter a denial." How could they permit themselves to make a claim that would necessitate knowledge as extensive as the scheme of the universe, when their knowledge of the total scheme of being is close to zero?

What proof exists to substantiate the claim that being is equivalent to matter and that the whole world of being consists of material entities? What scientist rejecting metaphysics has ever been able to found his denial on logic or proof, or to furnish evidence that beyond absolute non-being, nothing exists outside the sensory realm?

*****

Although science does not explicitly and definitively reject every unknown thing simply because it can have no access to it by means of its tools and instruments, patiently awaiting instead the day when it should be discovered, materialists do not even approach the question of the existence of God with doubt and hesitation; on the basis of their erroneous and hasty prejudices, they pronounce their judgment that the Creator does not exist.

Such persons establish certain criteria and standards for themselves and are not prepared to apply a different criterion established for a definite purpose in a given area. For example, they would never use the criteria applicable to a surface to measure a body, but when it comes to measuring the supra-sensory world, they try to measure God, the spirit, and inspiration, with the same tools they use to measure the material world. When they find themselves unable to gain any knowledge of the entities in question, they proceed to deny their existence.

Now, if a person imprisoned in empirical logic desires to accept the reality of the universe only to the extent permitted him by sensory experience and to deny whatever lies beyond that, he must recognize that this is a path he has chosen for himself; it is not the result of scientific investigation and experiment. This kind of pseudo-intellectualism arises from intellectual rebellion and an abandonment of one's original nature. The god that the natural scientist wishes vainly to "prove" with his tools and instruments is, in any event, no god at all in the view of those who worship God.

Lesson Four
Belief in the Reality of the Unseen
Involves More than God

One of the characteristics of the unique God to the knowledge and worship of Whom Prophets and religious leaders summon us is that He is utterly inaccessible to sense perception. In addition, He possesses the attributes of pre-eternity and post-eternity. Existing everywhere, He is nowhere. Throughout the world of nature and sensory being His manifestations have an objective existence and His will is everywhere manifest in the world of being, all the phenomena of nature declaring the power of that wise Essence.

Of course, such a being that man cannot perceive with his senses, that is not in any way colored by materiality, and that does not correspond to our normal experience and observation, is extremely difficult for us to imagine. Once the existence of a thing is difficult to imagine, it becomes easy to deny it.

Those who want to solve the question of existence of God within the framework of their own intellectual limitations and narrowness of vision ask how it is possible to believe in an unseen being. They overlook the fact that sense perception, being limited, can help man to know and perceive only one mode of being; it cannot discover other modes of being and penetrate all the dimensions of existence. Sensory organs do not permit us to advance a single step beyond the outer aspects of phenomena, in just the same way that the empirical sciences cannot carry human thought beyond the boundaries of the supra-sensory.

If man, through the application of scientific instruments and criteria, cannot perceive the existence of a thing, he cannot deny its existence simply because it is incompatible with material criteria, unless he disposes of some proof that the thing in question is impossible.

We discover the existence of an objective law from within the totality of phenomena that it is capable of interpreting. If, then, the establishment of scientific truth is possible only by means of direct sensation, the majority of scientific truths will have to be discarded, since many scientific facts cannot be perceived by means of sensory experience or testing.

*****

As far as the realities of the material world are concerned, no rational person will commonly regard his not seeing or not sensing a given thing in his everyday life as grounds enough to deny it. He will not condemn as non-existent whatever fails to enter the sphere of his sense perception. This same will hold true *a fortiori* of non-material realities.

When we are unable to establish the cause of something in a scientific experiment, this does not lead us to deny the law of causality. We say only that the cause is unknown to us because the law is independent of a given experiment; no experiment can lead to the negation of causality.

Is it not true that all the things we accept and believe to exist have an existence belonging to the same category as our own or as things that are visible to us? Can we see or feel everything in this material world? Is it only God we cannot see with our senses?

All materialists are aware that many of the things known to us consist of matters and realities that we cannot sense and with which we are not customarily familiar. There are many invisible beings in the universe. The progress of science and knowledge in the present age have uncovered numerous truths of this kind, and one of the richest chapters in scientific research is the transformation of matter into energy.

When the beings and bodies that are visible in this world wish to produce energy, they are compelled to change their original aspect and transform it into energy. Now is this energy—the axis on which turn many of the motions and changes of the universe—visible or tangible?

We know that energy is a source of power, but the essence of energy still remains a mystery. Take electricity on which so much of our science, civilization and life depend. No physicist in his laboratory—or anyone else, for that matter, dealing with electrical tools and appliances—can see electricity itself or feel and touch its weight or softness. No one can directly perceive the passage of electricity through a wire; he can only perceive the existence of a current by using the necessary equipment.

Modern physics tells us that the things of which we have sense perception are firm, solid and stable, and there is no visible energy in their motions. But despite outward appearances, what we, in fact, see and perceive is a mass of atoms that are neither firm nor solid nor stable; all things are nothing other than transformation, change and motion. What our sense organs imagine to be stable and motionless lack all stability and permanence and immobility; motion, change and development embrace them all, without this being perceptible to us by way of direct sensory observation.

The air that surrounds us has a considerable weight and exerts a constant pressure on the body; everyone bears a pressure of 16,000 kilograms of air. But we do not feel any discomfort because the pressure of the air is neutralized by the inward pressure of the body. This established scientific fact was unknown until the time of Galileo and Pascal, and even now our senses cannot perceive it.[6]

The attributes assigned to natural factors by scientists on the basis of sensory experiments and rational deductions cannot be directly perceived. For example, radio waves are present everywhere and yet nowhere. There is no locus that is free of the attractive force of some material body, but this in no way detracts from its existence or lessens its substance.

Concepts such as justice, beauty, love, hatred, enmity, wisdom, that make up our mental universe, do not have a visible and clear-cut existence or the slightest physical aspect; nonetheless, we regard them as realities. Man does not know the essence of electricity, of radio waves, or energy, of electrons and neutrons; he perceives their existence only through their results and effects.

*****

Life very clearly exists; we cannot possibly deny it. But how can we measure it , and by what means can we measure the speed of thought and imagination?

From all this it is quite clear that to deny whatever lies beyond our vision and hearing is contrary to logic and the conventional principles of reason. Why do the deniers of God fail to apply the common principles of science to the particular question of the existence of a power ruling over nature?

A certain materialist of Egypt went to Mecca in order to engage in debate, and there he met Imam Sadiq, upon whom be peace.

The Imam said, "Begin your questioning."

The Egyptian said nothing.

The Imam: "Do you accept that the earth has an above and a below?"

The Egyptian: "Yes."

The Imam: "So how do you know what is below the earth?"

The Egyptian: "I do not know, but I think there is nothing below the earth."

The Imam: "Imagining is a sign of impotence when confronted with what you cannot be certain of. Now tell me, have you ever been up in the skies?"

The Egyptian: "No."

The Imam: "How strange it is that you have not been to the West or to the East, that you have not descended below the earth or flown up to the heavens, or passed beyond them to know what lies there, but nonetheless you deny what exists there. Would any wise man deny the reality of what he is ignorant of? And you deny the existence of the Creator because you cannot see him with your eyes."

The Egyptian: "No one talked to me before in this way."

The Imam: "So, in fact, you have doubts concerning the existence of God; you think He may exist and He may not exist?"

The Egyptian: "Perhaps so."

The Imam: "O man, the hands of one who does not know are empty of all proof; the ignorant can never possess any kind of evidence. Be well aware that we never have any kind of doubt or hesitation concerning the existence of God. Do you not see the sun and the moon, the day and the night, regularly alternating and following a fixed course? If they have any power of their own, let them depart from their course and not return. Why do they constantly return? If they are free in their alternation and rotation, why does the night not become day and the day not become night? I swear by God that they have no free choice in their motions; it is He Who causes these phenomena to follow a fixed course; it is He Who commands them; and to Him alone belongs all greatness and splendor."

The Egyptian: "You speak truly."

The Imam: "If you imagine that nature and time carry men forward, then why do they not carry them backwards? And if they carry them backwards, why do they not carry them forward?"

"Know that the heavens and the earth are subject to His Will. Why do the heavens not collapse onto the earth? Why are the layers of the earth not overturned and why do they not mount up to the heavens? Why do those who live on the earth not adhere to each other?"

The Egyptian: "God Who is the Lord and Master of the heavens and earth protects them from collapse and destruction."

"The words of the Imam had now caused the light of faith to shine on the heart of the Egyptian; he submitted to the truth and accepted Islam."[7]

Let us not forget that we are imprisoned in the framework of matter and its dimensions; we cannot imagine an absolute being with our customary habits of thought. If we tell a villager that a great and populous city exists called London, he will conceive in his mind of some big village, maybe ten times bigger than his own, and the same with respect to its buildings, the way people dress, their way of life and dealings with each other. He will assume that the characteristics of people everywhere are the same as in his own village.

The only thing we can tell him to correct the unrealistic way he thinks is that London is indeed a place of settlement, but not of the kind you imagine, and its characteristics are not of the same kind you see in your own village.

What we can say concerning God is that God exists, and that He possesses life, power and knowledge, but His existence and knowledge and power are not of the kind familiar to us. In this way we can, to some extent, escape the restrictions placed on our understanding. For the materialist, too, it is impossible to conceive of the essence of primary matter.

Although it appears that sense objects are the things we know most clearly and precisely, we cannot rely exclusively on such objects in scientific and philosophical matters. Laying aside all fanatical attitudes, we must assess the true nature of sense objects and the degree to which they can aid men in uncovering the truth. Otherwise, they will mislead us, because sense perception relates only to certain qualities of the external aspect of sense objects. It cannot perceive the totality of those qualities or the essence and mere substance of sense objects, let alone non-sensing objects.

The eye that is the surest means for the perception of reality is, in many cases, unable to show reality to us. It can observe lights only when their wave length is not less than 4% microns and more than 8% microns, and, therefore, it cannot see lights higher than violet or lower than red. In addition, the errors made by sense perception form an important section in books on psychology: the eye is known to commit numerous errors.

The colors we recognize in the external world are, in fact, not colors. They are vibrations on different wave lengths. Our visual sense experiences have different wave lengths of light in accordance with its own particular mechanism as colors. In other words, what we perceive by means of our senses is limited by the structure and capacity of those senses. For example, the structure of the visual sense in certain animals such as cows and cats causes them to see monotone external reality as colored. From the viewpoint of scientific analysis, the nature of the mechanism in man's visual sense that permits him to see colors is not entirely clear and the theories put forward so far are all hypothetical. The question of man's ability to see colors is obscure and complex.

In order to see how the sense of touch may be deceived, you can fill three bowls with water: the first with very hot water, the second with very cold water, and the third with lukewarm water. Then place one hand in hot water and the other in cold water, and leave them there for a time. Then place them both in lukewarm water , and you will see to your great surprise that you experience contradictory sensations. One hand will tell you that the lukewarm water is extremely cold, and the other will proclaim that it is extremely hot. Of course, the water is one and the same, and its temperature is known.

Now, reason and logic say that it is not possible for water to be both cold and hot at the same time, to have two contradictory attributes. It is the sense of touch that is at fault, having lost its self-control as a result of the two bowls of water in which the hands were immersed. What it feels is at variance with the truth, and reason and the mind point out its error.

This being the case, how can we rely on sense perception without the guidance of the intellect and mental criteria? Is there any way to protect ourselves against the errors of sense perception other than rational judgment?

Once someone asked the Commander of the Believers, upon whom be peace, "Have you seen your Lord?"

He answered: "I will never worship a Lord whom I cannot see."

The man then asked: "How did you see him? Explain it to us."

He replied, "Woe upon you! No one has ever seen Him with the physical eye, but hearts filled with the truth of faith have contemplated Him."•

It is then the judgment of reason that is entrusted with the task of correcting the errors of sense perception, and the source of that judgment lies beyond the sensory realm.

*****

Sense perception cannot, therefore, yield a realistic vision; its only value is practical. Those who rely exclusively on sense perception in their investigations will never be able to solve the problems of existence and the riddle of creation.

From our assessment of the competence of sense perception, we reach the conclusion that even in the empirical, sensory realm, it is unable to bestow alone certain knowledge on man and to guide him to the truth. *A fortiori*, the same is true of matters that are beyond sensory perception.

The followers of metaphysics are convinced that in just the same way that experiment and testing are the method of investigation and cognition to be followed in the sensory sciences, it is intellection that is the means of discovering the truth in metaphysical matters.

The Primality of the Life Principle

Science says it is life that creates life. The life of animate beings is possible only by means of generation, procreation and the reproduction of species. No single cell has yet been discovered that was born from lifeless matter. Even the lowest forms of living being, such as fungi and parasites, cannot come into existence and grow unless a cause that itself partakes of life is to be found in its environment.

According to the testimony of science, the earth went through long periods in which there was no possibility of life because of the extreme heat prevailing. No vegetation was to be seen on the face of the planet and there were no rivers or springs. The atmosphere was full of molten metals and volcanic eruptions. Later, when the crust of the earth began to cool, only inorganic matter could be found there for millions of years. In short, throughout the tumultuous changes that took place on the surface of the earth, there was no trace of life on it. How, then, did life suddenly gush forth?

There is no doubt life came into being some time after the appearance of the earth; how long that process took and how it came about is not known.

For centuries researchers have been striving in their laboratories to uncover the mystery of life, this truly remarkable phenomenon, but they have not yet come any closer to solving the riddle.

One researcher writes in the book *Distant Worlds*, "What a bewitching word is life! Did existence come into being from non-existence? Can organic matter emerge from inorganic matter? Or is some powerful and creative hand at work? It is sometimes suggested that life may have come to our planet from other heavenly bodies, because when the lowest forms of life—the seeds of vegetable microbes—swimming in the atmosphere of a heavenly body rise to a great elevation, the rays of the sun may carry them by means of pressure into space, so that they ultimately reach the surface of another heavenly body where they flourish and develop.

"This hypothesis does not represent the slightest progress in the solution of the great riddle, because if the hypothesis be true, we still do not know how life appeared, whether on one of the planets in the solar system or one of the Great Dog stars. Just as a clock is not made by heaping together springs, cogs, bolts and levers, so, too, the creation of life is not possible in the absence of a heart—i.e., that which sets life in motion—and a summons that proclaims 'come to life!' "

We know that matter in and of itself lacks life and that no material element possesses life unaided. Thus life cannot be supposed to proceed from the harmonious compounding of the atoms that make up matter. The question arises why living matter cannot repeat itself other than by procreation and reproduction of the species. Chemical actions and reactions are constantly underway in inanimate bodies without any trace of life being reflected in them. To say that matter is inclined to compounding and that life suddenly emerged in the course of its development and evolution is to describe the living and vital phenomena we sensorially observe; it is not to explain the origin of life and its cause.

Moreover, the particles of matter were not originally incompatible with each other; a cause must, therefore, have operated to bring about the compounding of some of them and to prevent the compounding of others. And what is the cause for some particles being endowed with life and others deprived of it?

The only thing to result from the compounding of two or more elements is that each element gives to the other some of the properties it possesses; how should it make a gift of something it does not possess? The elements acquire a common property as a result of compounding, a property that cannot go beyond the properties that each possess, but life with its unique character bears no similarity to the properties of matter. Life displays itself in ways of which matter is incapable, and in many respects, indeed, life dominates matter. Although life appears to be dependent on matter, matter being the mould which receives it, motion, will and, ultimately, perception and knowledge appear in matter only when life casts its rays upon it. It is, therefore, unjustifiable to attempt to interpret life in terms of chemical reactions.

What factor is it that manufactures cells in numerous different varieties and with different programs and then inserts them in a planned form? It prepares reproductive cells that transfer the characteristics and peculiarities of fathers to their offspring, without the slightest error occurring in the performance of that function.

We see that life cells have certain particular characteristics in their composition, among which are repair, reconstruction, preservation of the species, and the capacity for variation.

Every cell in man functions at the required time and in the required manner. The distribution of labor and function among cells is remarkable. They are distributed in the quantity needed to assure growth of the body, and every cell goes to its appointed place in the brain, the lungs, the liver, the heart and the kidneys. Once the cells have taken up their appointed positions, they do not fail for an instant in performing their vital functions; they disperse and repel superfluous and useless matter and preserve exactly their proper volume.

To ascribe this remarkable classification which has the purpose of forming, in due proportion, the limbs and organs needed by

animate beings to mechanical and unconscious factors is a completely inadequate interpretation. What freely thinking person
would accept such illogicality?

Life is, then, a light which shines from lofty horizons on
material entities that have the capacity to receive it; it sets them in
motion and puts each intelligently in its particular locus.

It is the guiding will of the Creator, His power to decide in a
way that ensures movement and development toward perfection,
and His comprehensive and far-reaching wisdom, that bestow the
great miracle of life, with all its properties, on lifeless matter. A man
who is aware of the truth sees a constant thread of life running
through the changing and moving substance of matter. He contem-
plates God in His aspect of continuous creation and origination, His
ceaseless impelling of all things toward perfection.

Lesson Five
The Manifestations of God in Nature

The world of matter and nature, conceived as a created whole, is the best, clearest and most universal evidence for the knowledge of God. The wise will of that Eternal Principle can be discovered in the very processes of material change. It is apparent that His eternal rays bestow life and sustenance on all beings, and that all of creation derives both its existence and its advancement from Him.

To study the different beings in the universe, the mysteries of the book of creation, the pages of which all bear witness to the operation of a lofty intelligence in its creation, provides, then, evidence on which to base knowledge and belief in a wise Creator Whose power is but slightly manifested in the order of beings for all their splendor and vastness. It is, moreover, a simple and straight-forward proof that lacks the complexity and weightiness of philo-sophical evidence. It is a path for study and contemplation that is open to all; everyone can benefit from it, both thinkers and scholars and the simple masses of humanity.

Everyone, to the extent permitted by his capacity and vision, can see in all the phenomena of creation indications of connected-ness, harmony, and purposefulness, and find in every one of the countless particles of creation a firm proof for the existence of the source of being.

The complete adaption of every species of animal to its condi-tions of life is a great sign of God; each has been created with all the particular instruments needed for its conditions of life.

Moses, the one who spoke with God, peace be upon our Prophet and him , made use of this proof in order to demonstrate the existence of God to the Pharaoh. The Pharaoh said to Moses and his brother: *"Who is your Lord?"* Moses, peace be upon our Prophet and him, replied, *"Our Lord is the one Who endowed all things with a particular form of creation."* (20:49)

Likewise, Imam Sadiq, peace be upon him, said to Mufaddal, "Look carefully at the structure of the bird's creation; see how it has been created light and small in volume to enable it to fly. It was given only two legs instead of the four given to other animals and only four of the five toes they have on each foot. Birds have slim, pointed breasts to enable them to fend the air easily and fly in every direction. The long legs of the bird fit easily beneath its tail and its wings, and its whole body is covered with feathers so that air might penetrate them and aid it to fly. Since the food of birds consists of seeds and the flesh of animals that they consume without chewing, they have no need of teeth. Instead, God created for birds a hard and sharp beak that cannot break when tearing off meat or suffer injury when gathering seeds. To enable this creature to digest the food it has not chewed, it has been given a powerful digestive system and a warm body. Furthermore, birds reproduce by laying eggs so they can remain light enough to fly; if their offspring were to grow in their stomachs, they would become too heavy to fly."

Then the Imam referred to a general law, saying, "Thus all the peculiarities of a bird's creation conform to its environment and its manner of life."⁹

The question of animal speech—the means by which animals communicate with each other—is another divine sign. They possess a special kind of language that enables them to communicate with each other.

The Noble Quran thus relates the story of an ant addressing the Prophet Solomon, peace be upon our Prophet and him, *"An ant said, 'O ants, enter your dwellings lest Solomon and his army unwittingly trample you underfoot."* (27:18)

Modern scientists have discovered a sophisticated system of communication among the animals that is more complex and precise than our own system of communication. Crissy Morrison writes, "If we put a female moth next to the window of our room, it emits soft signals that a male moth picks up from an incredible distance and it sends its own signals in return. However much you may wish to disturb this communication, you will be unable to do so. Does this weak creature carry some kind of transmitter, or does the male moth have a receiver concealed in his antennae?

"A cricket rubs its legs together, and the sound can be heard up to a kilometer away on a quiet, still night. In order to summon its mate, the male cricket sets sixty tons of air in motion and the female cricket sends a warm response to his wooings by some physical means, although apparently no sound is audible from her.

"Before the invention of radio, scientists used to imagine that animals communicated with each other by means of smell. Supposing this hypothesis to be true, it would still be something of a miracle, because the smell would have to move through the air to reach the nostrils of the female insect. This is quite apart from the question of whether a wind is blowing or not and how the female insect is to pick up the smell and tell where it is coming from, enabling her to know where her suitor is located.

"Today, thanks to highly complex mechanical means, we have gained the ability to communicate with each other over great distances. Radio is a remarkable invention, enabling us to communicate with each other instantaneously. But the use of this invention is dependent on a wire and our being present in a certain place. The moth is still way ahead of us."[10]

Choosing the empirical sciences as a means of studying the infinite mysteries of the world has another advantage in addition to lying within the reach of everyone. It is that awareness of the wonders of creation and the order prevailing in it which naturally links man to the God Who has created it; such awareness displays to man the attributes of perfection, knowledge and limitless power that characterize the Creator and Source of all being.

This precise order indicates an aim, a plan, broad and extensive wisdom. What creativity, what power, what knowledge He has invested in all the world of being, in the smallest and the greatest of His creation alike—in the earth, in the atmosphere, in the heavenly bodies, in the heart of stones, in the heart of atoms!

When we speak of "order" it should be understood that the concept of order is applicable to a phenomenon when its different parts are somehow interrelated in such a way that they harmoniously pursue a specific aim; the collaboration of the parts with each other must also have been taken into account.

Although those who deny the existence of order in the universe generally do not deny the existence of an active cause (since they accept the law of causality), what is meant by the principle of mutual acquaintance in nature is the ultimate cause, and this—implying as it does the intervention of aim and purpose in natural phenomena—they do reject.

In numerous of its verses, the Noble Quran invites men to ponder on the order of creation so that the mass of people should be able, in the simplest way possible, to become aware of the existence of the Unique Creator.

These are some of the verses in question: *"In the creation of the heavens and the earth, in the alternation of the night and the day, in the sailing of ships through the ocean for the profit of mankind; in the rain which God sends down from the skies and the life He gives therewith to a land that is dead; in the beasts of all kinds that He scatters through the earth; in the change of the winds and the clouds which they trail like their slaves between the sky and the earth—in all of these matters, there are for the wise, clear proofs of the knowledge and power of the Creator."* (2:164)

"God it is, that Pure Essence, that has raised the heavens without any pillar, as you see, and then adorned His throne in the midst of creation with perfect power. He has subjected the sun and the moon to His will so that each of them rotates in due course. He has imposed firm order on the affairs of the world and set forth the signs of His power with detailed proofs, that you may believe with certainty in the meeting with your Lord." (13:2)

"He it is Who spread out the earth and raised the mountains upon it. He made the rivers course and brought forth every kind of fruit, and He created all things in pairs. He covered the bright day with the dark night. Certainly in these matters are clear proofs for the thoughtful of the power of the Creator." (13:3)

If we accept and have recourse to every theory that has been put forward by the specialists and researchers, even the theory of evolution concerning the appearance of the various species found in the world, none of the theories in question will be comprehensible without the presence of an absolute power, the intervention of a will, an awareness, and a final purpose and aim. Gradual creation within the system of nature also clearly displays the intervention of will and awareness in its processes; all the stages in the movement and progress of nature have been based on a very exact choice and calculation, and nature has never diverged in the slightest in millions of years from its ordained path.

It is true that in the initial stages of deriving proof for the existence of God from the orderliness of the universe, use is made of empirical data, and that some parts of the argument are constructed with the help of the senses, the study of nature and empirical observation. However, in reality, the argument is not an empirical one but rather a rational one, guiding us away from nature toward the transcendent reality that lies beyond nature. Empirical proofs concern the relationship between two parts of nature, each of which must be sensorially perceptible to permit the relationship between the two phenomena to be established.

When we estimate the degree of knowledge and awareness of a person by examining his works and achievements, we are not engaged in an empirical discovery, for the degree of knowledge and intelligence of a person is not a tangible quantity for us subject to direct experimentation on our part. Of course, man directly experiences will, intelligence, and thought within his own being, but he does not have a similar awareness of their existence in others; they are inaccessible to him.

It is through the works and achievements of men that we become aware of the existence of intelligence and thought in them, although there is no empirical proof of their existence in them. Now the discovery of intelligence in others by way of their works and achievements rests on a rational proof, not an empirical deduction in the sense of intelligence and its workings being directly susceptible to direct examination so that their interrelations might be discovered. This discovery also does not rest on a logical comparison in the sense of positing an identity between one individual and all others.

Given, then, that the recognition of thought and intelligence in men does not take place by way of empirical proof, it is obvious that the argument of orderliness in the universe and its connection with the divine essence also does not belong to the category of empirical proofs.

*****

From another point of view, since man is not the creator of nature but a part of it, his actions in the world of nature represent the establishment of a relationship between different parts of that world.

The aim and the purpose pursued by man in the compounding of a whole series of material elements (as, for example, in constructing a building, a car, or a factory) relate to his own being; that is, the ultimate purpose and aim is the maker himself, not the thing made. The relationship between the parts of the things made is, therefore, a non-natural relationship; by establishing that relationship, the maker wishes to attain his own purposes and to relive his own deficiencies, for all the efforts of man are a movement from potentiality to actuality and deficiency to perfection.

However, these two characteristics do not apply to the relationship between created beings and God. The relationship between the different parts of God's works is not a non-natural one, and the purpose of the created phenomenon does not relate to the Creator. Put differently, the aims of God's acts all relate to the acts themselves, not to the Agent, for God's wisdom necessitates that He should cause all beings to attain their perfection.

If in the course of developing the argument of the orderliness of the universe we attempt to prove the existence of a maker similar to the human maker, the divine maker will, in reality, also be a created being on the level of man; proving the existence of such a maker is an entirely different matter from proving the existence of the Maker and Creator of all being. From a scientific point of view, the self-origination of matter is impossible; the Marxist theory that the material world is constantly evolving and advancing toward higher states is clearly contradictory to scientific data and the realities of nature. All development and motion in the mineral realm is due either to the intervention of a will external to matter or to attraction, interchange, and compounding with other bodies.

In the vegetable world, development, growth and increase occur as the result of rainfall, sunshine and obtaining the necessary materials from the soil. The same is the case in the animal world, except that there the factor of volitional movement toward what is useful and necessary must be added.

In all the instances just mentioned, there is a clear cooperation between things and creatures, on the one hand, and factors external to them, on the other. In accordance with the particular properties innate in each being and the laws and formulae to which it is subject, it is incapable of disobeying the commands that have been engraved in its being.

The realities that man perceives by way of his senses have certain particular properties. We sense clearly that beings in this world are subject to change and impermanence. Throughout the period of its existence, any material being is either proceeding along the path of growth and development or advancing toward decay and decline. In short, no material being on the plane of existence remains fixed and unchanging.

Finiteness is another property of a sensory existent. From the smallest particle to the biggest galaxy, all things are in need of space and time; it is simply that certain things occupy a greater space or a longer time, and others, a shorter time and a smaller space. Moreover, all material beings are relative from the point of view of their very existence as well as the properties they possess; whatever attributes such as power, magnificence, beauty and wisdom we ascribe to things, we do so in comparison to something else.

Dependence and conditionality are also among the characteristics of these beings. The existence of any being we may conceive is dependent and conditional on other factors, and it, therefore, stands in need of them. No material thing can be found in the world that relies entirely upon itself, that has no need of anything other than itself. Neediness and dependence, therefore, circumscribe all material beings.

Man's intelligence and thought are able to transcend the veils of outward appearance, unlike his senses, and to penetrate the depths and inner dimension of being; they cannot accept that existence should be confined to relative, finite, changing and dependent beings. On the contrary, the power of thought clearly recognizes the necessity of the existence, beyond the observable realm, of a stable, absolute and self-subsistent reality upon which all other beings rely and depend. This reality is present in all times and at all places; were it not to be present, the totality of the world would cease to exist and would lose all share of being.

Once we see the dependency of the created world and realize that no phenomenon can exist unaided, we conclude that there is a Necessary Existent, for we are compelled to ask, "Upon what is every phenomenon ultimately dependent?"

If we answer, "On another body," then we must ask, "On what is that body, in turn, dependent?" If, then, the answer is given, "On a thing the nature of which is unknown to us," the question arises, "Is that thing simple or compound?"

If it is said to be compound, then we reply that a compound is also dependent on its parts, since first the parts must exist in order for the compound to come into being. Since nature is a compound, it cannot be the Necessary Existent.

We are, therefore, compelled to say that the first cause must be simple; it must also be coterminous with the Necessary Existent, since the chain of causality cannot continue indefinitely.

The totality of the world is, then, in need of a reality that is independent and upon which all conditional, finite and relative phenomena depend. All things need that reality to fill them with being, and all beings possess a sign of its infinite life, knowledge, power and wisdom. They, thus, permit us to gain valuable knowledge concerning that reality and enable every intelligent, curious person to deduce the existence of a Creator.

*****

The mutual dependence of matter and the laws of being in no way points to the independence of matter. On the contrary, the different phenomena that arise from matter, together with their close interrelatedness, indicate that matter, in its mode of existence, is compelled to accept and follow certain laws and norms that impel it to order and harmony. Existence depends on two basic factors: matter and orderliness, which are closely interrelated and give birth to a coherent and harmonious world.

Some people regard matter as independent and imagine that it has itself gained this freedom and elaborated the laws that rule over it. But how can they believe that hydrogen and oxygen, electrons and protons, should first produce themselves, then be the source for all other beings, and finally decree the laws that regulate themselves and the rest of the material world?

Materialism imagines that lowly objects are the source for the emergence of higher objects without troubling to ascertain whether the higher, in fact, exists at the level of the lower. If lowly matter is unable—even at the highest stage of its development, namely thought and reflection—either to create itself or to violate any of the laws that rule over it, it follows ineluctably that it is unable to create other beings and the laws regulating them. How, then, can it be believed that lowly matter should engage in the creation and origination of higher beings or have the power to bestow existence on lofty phenomena?

In the new science of systems, the principle has been established that systems comprising living elements that have an aim or systems organized externally on the basis of a given program, may develop in the direction of expansion, greater orderliness and improvement. However, all systems, whether simple or compound, need to be aided by and interrelated with factors external to themselves; they are unable to construct themselves. No system or substance in the world will be able to create or to will a moving and developing organ unless it enjoys a measure of will power and consciousness.

Based on the law of probabilities, the result of universal independent motivation could be only dispersal and anarchy, tending to a uniform death.

The law of probabilities also decisively refutes the appearance of the world by way of accident, considering it irrational and impossible. Even calculations based on the mathematical law of probabilities confirm the necessity of correct guidance and planning for the world, in accordance with a precise program and a conscious will.

The law of probabilities deals, in fact, a decisive blow to those who believe in theory of the accidental origination of the universe. If we attempt to apply the theory of accident to a simple system or to small numbers, its applicability is not impossible, although extremely unlikely. But it is inconceivable that one should ever chance on a geometric accident expressing the firm orderliness and harmony that prevail in the complex system of the world. Partial and simple changes in the order of existence are also unable to explain the transformation of the world, the coalescing of diverse elements, and the compounding of fundamental atoms to form a harmonious compound.

If nature was once engaged autonomously in composition and formation, why does it not now display any initiative in the direction of changing itself further; why does it no longer exhibit profound, automatic change?

Even slight and simple occurrences in the world result in the creation of remarkable images that are harmonious and consonant with the aim of creation. This is itself an indication of the truth that behind all the stupendous changes, a conscious and powerful force is engaged in creating and producing the wondrous system of the universe: it gives shape to the remarkable crystallization of the world of creation and traces out the plan and order of being.

*****

The harmony and interconnectedness of millions of natural phenomena and their relationship to life can be explained on the basis of one hypothesis only—namely that we conceive of a Creator for this vast system Who has established the diverse elements of life on this globe by means of a limitless and infinite power and drawn up a program for each of those elements. This hypothesis is in conformity with the harmonious links that we see embedded in a phenomenon.

If we do not accept this hypothesis, how likely is it that such harmony should have come about—accidentally and without purpose—among the variegated orders of being? How could it be believed that matter should itself be the origin of millions of attributes and characteristics and thus be the equivalent of the purposeful, wise and all-knowing Creator?

If the world of being did not exist, with all its wonders that bedazzle the intellect and the splendor of which human knowledge cannot fully comprehend, and if the universe consisted simply of a mono-cellular being, still the possibility that such a slight and insignificant entity, together with the order prevailing over it and the necessary conditions and materials, should come into existence as a mere chance, a possibility, an accident, such a possibility represents, according to the Swiss biologist Charles Unguy, so minute a figure as to be mathematically inconceivable.

*****

All the particles of existent beings are subject, both in their internal structure and in their interrelations, to a well-established order. Their composition and their relations with each other are such that they aid each other to advance along their respective paths to the aims that lie before them. Benefiting from the relationship they have with all other beings and from their exchange of influence in them as determined by their own composition, they are able to advance toward their aim and destination.

The principal accomplishment of the material sciences is to identify the external aspects and qualities of the world; to identify the essence and true nature of created beings and phenomena lies beyond the grasp of those sciences.

For example, the utmost achievement of which an astronomer is capable is to know whether the billions of spheres in the heavens are fixed and stationary by virtue of centrifugal force or whether they are continuing to rotate while a force of attraction prevents them from colliding with each other and maintains their equilibrium. He may also measure their distance from the earth and their speed and volume by means of scientific instruments. However, the final result of all this knowledge and experimentation does not extend beyond the interpretation of the external and superficial aspects of creation, for the astronomer is unable to perceive the true nature of the attractive force, the essence of the centrifugal force or the manner in which they and the system they serve came into being.

Scientists can interpret a machine without being aware of the interpretation of the motive power. The natural sciences are similarly incapable of interpreting and analyzing the millions of truths that are embedded in nature and in the human person.

Man has delved into the heart of the atom but has been unable to solve the complex and obscure mysteries of a single living atom. In short, it is these bastions of mystery that the champions of the natural sciences have been unable to conquer.

One of the wonders of creation is the mutual harmony existing between two phenomena that are not contemporaneous with each other. This harmony is of such a nature that the needs of a phenomenon that has not yet come into being are already provided for in the structure of another phenomenon.

The best example of this kind of harmony can be seen in the relationship between mother and child. Among humans and other mammals, as soon as the female becomes pregnant and as the foetus grows in the womb, the mammary gland that produces milk—a pleasant and comprehensive form of nurture—sets to work under the influence of special hormones. As the foetus grows, this nutritive substance increases in quantity so that when the foetus is on the threshold of birth and is ready to step forth into the broad and limitless world, the nutriment needed by the child and suited to all its bodily needs stands ready.

This ready-made substance is perfectly attuned to the still undeveloped digestive system of the infant. It is stored in a hidden depot—the breast of the mother, a depot with which the mother was equipped years before the infant took shape. In order to facilitate the feeding of the newly-born infant, small, delicate holes are placed in the tip of the breast—itself of a size to fit in the mouth of the infant—so that the milk should not flow directly into the mouth of one who does not have the power to swallow it. Instead, the infant draws the daily sustenance it needs from that depot by sucking.

As the newly born infant grows, changes appear in the milk that are linked to his age. It is for this reason that physicians believe the suckling of a newly born infant by wet-nurses who have not born a child in some time to be inadvisable.

Here the question arises: is not the provision for the needs of a being made in the structure of one being for the needs of another being that does not yet exist, something planned and foreseen on the basis of wisdom and exactitude? Is not this provision for the future, this subtle and wondrous interrelation between two beings, the work of a powerful and all-wise power? Is it not a clear sign of the intervention of an infinite power, a great designer and planner, whose purpose is the continuation of life and the growth of all phenomena toward perfection?

We know well that the precise calculations which we can see underlying all machines and industrial tools are the result of the talents and ideas that went into their planning and construction. Similarly, based on our objective observations we can reach the general philosophical conclusion that wherever order and assembly based on balance and calculation are to be observed, will, intelligence and thought should also be sought.

The same precision that can be observed in industrial machines is to be seen to a higher and more remarkable degree in natural beings and their composition. Indeed, the degree of planning and organization visible in nature is at such a high level that the precision expended by man on his own creations cannot in any way be compared with it.

When, without hesitation, we recognize that our industrial order is the product of thought and of will, ought we not perceive the operation of infinite intelligence, will and knowledge behind the precise planning of nature?

*****

In the present age, the science of medicine has reached a degree of progress that permits it to remove a kidney from within the human body and implant it in the body of a person whose kidney has stopped functioning and who is on the verge of death. This advance is assuredly not the result of one physician's labors alone; it draws on the legacy of several millennia.

A transplant operation is then the final stage in a long process, the preliminary stages of which were accomplished by earlier scientists: the ideas and insights of scientists had to accumulate for several thousand years before a kidney transplant could take place.

Is it possible that this result could have been attained without knowledge? Plainly not: powerful human brains had to labor for several millennia for the transplanting of kidneys to be made possible.

Now let us pose another question. Which requires the more knowledge and science: the changing of a tire on the wheel of an automobile—a task which admittedly calls for a certain technical skill—or the manufacture of the tire itself? Which is more significant: the making of the tire or changing it?

Although a kidney transplant is a medically significant procedure, it resembles changing the tire on the wheel of an automobile; it fades into insignificance when compared with the structure of the kidney itself and the mysteries, subtleties and calculations that it contains.

What realistic scientist, sincerely given to seeking the truth could claim today that while a kidney transplant is the result of centuries of continuous scientific research and experimentation, the structure of the kidney itself reveals no trace of a creative intelligence and will, being the product of mere nature—nature which has no more knowledge or awareness than a kindergarten pupil?

Is it not more logical to posit the existence of intelligence, will and planning in the creation of and ordering of the world than to attribute creativity to matter which lacks intelligence, thought, consciousness and the power to innovate?

Belief in the existence of a wise creator is without doubt more logical than faith in the creativity of matter, which has neither perception, consciousness, nor the ability to plan; we cannot attribute to matter all the properties and attributes of intelligence that we see in the world and the ordering will that it displays.

Mufaddal said to Imam Sadiq (upon whom be peace!): "Master, some men imagine that the order and precision we see in the world are the work of nature."

The Imam responded: "Ask them whether nature performs all its precisely calculated functions in accordance with knowledge, thought and power of its own. If they say that nature possesses knowledge and power, what is there to prevent them from affirming the eternal divine essence and confessing the existence of that supreme principle? If, on the other hand, they say that nature performs its tasks regularly and correctly without knowledge and will, then it follows that these wise functions and precise, well-calculated laws are the work of an all-knowing and wise creator. That which they call nature is, in fact, a law and a custom appointed by the hand of divine power to rule over creation."[11]

The Subtleties of Nature

Consider a malarial mosquito. There is no need to use a microscope; through the customary use of the naked eye you will be able to perceive the precise and complex order contained in that insignificant object.

Within this delicate object there exists a complete set of members and senses, remarkable for their precision: a digestive system, a circulatory system, a nervous system, a respiratory system. The mosquito possesses a fully equipped laboratory: with wonderful precision and speed it processes all the materials it needs. Compare with it a scientific laboratory: For all the human and economic resources devoted to it, it can never attain the speed, precision and exactitude of the contemptible laboratory of the mosquito. How much time, reflection and intelligence are needed, for example, to manufacture a cure for the mosquito's sting!

When so much planning, thought and precision are needed for man to perform such a task, are not the subtlety, exactitude and orderliness observable in the world a proof of origination deriving from the intelligence, creative planning and far-reaching wisdom of the creator? Is it at all feasible to regard all the precise geometry, functioning and movement of the universe as the outcome of matter in its ignorance? We proclaim most affirmatively that the phenomena of creation express order and regularity; they do not proclaim purposelessness, anarchy and disorder.

If we occasionally perceive weak points in nature this does not imply inadequacy or defect in the vast book of creation. Our thought and perception are unable to soar and take flight, and the reach of our intelligence is too short to understand all the mysteries and enigmas of the universe. Our intellect cannot discern all the aims and goals of existence.

If we are unable to understand the function of a small screw in a great machine, does this give us the right to accuse and condemn its designer as ignorant? Or is that the horizon of our gaze is too narrow to encompass the true aim and purpose of the machine?

Accident cannot perform the task of knowledge, knowledge, moreover, that is never commingled with ignorance in any way. If, as the materialists imagine, the world of nature did not arise from knowledge and will (despite the signs of creativity and inventiveness apparent in its every phenomenon) then man, too, in order to attain his purposes would have to abandon his advance on the path of knowledge and imprison himself in ignorance in order to conform to the ignorance of nature itself.

The reality that guides and directs the functioning of the world with such regularity and orderliness possesses an aim, purpose and will that cannot be denied. It cannot be supposed that the ceaseless process of action and reaction advances in a fixed direction without the intervention and supervision of an intelligence.

After years of careful planning and exhausting labor, biochemists have succeeded in discovering certain experimental organisms on a very simple and primitive level from which all trace of life is absent. This scientific triumph was regarded as very valuable and received with great enthusiasm in scientific circles, and nobody claimed that this highly deficient and primitive laboratory creation had come into being as the result of chance, without direction, planning and precision.

This being the case, those who ascribe all the beings in the vast system of the universe, together with their complex and mysterious properties to the blind and unconscious forces of matter, are, in reality, doing violence and injustice to logic and human intelligence and waging open war on the truth.

Give your attention for a minute to a typesetter in a printing house. He expends great care and attention when he is setting the letters required for one page of a book, but when he reviews his work, he comes across small errors arising from some slight inattention. Were the typesetter to take a handful of letters and scatter them over the plate instead of carefully arraying them in rows, is it at all possible that the resulting page should be correct in its contents and free of error?

It would be still more absurd to claim that a hundred kilograms of molten lead, forced through a tube, should emerge in the form of ready made letters; that a fierce tempest should then pick up those letters and arrange them in a particular and regular order on thousands of metal plates; and that these plates should result in the printing of a thousand-page book containing numerous precise scientific discussions and attractive, alluring expressions, all this without the slightest error occurring.

Could anyone support such a theory?

What do the materialists who deny God have to say concerning the emergence of the variegated forms of the letters of creation and the precise and complex relations that regulate the heavenly bodies, natural creation and all material objects? Are the letters of creation (i.e., the atoms and the particles that comprise them) in any way lesser than the letters used in printing? Is it in any way acceptable that these orderly, meaningful letters, this precise and well-organized geometry, the astounding forms depicted in the book of creation, should be the work of ignorance and aimlessness? That a great and wise power, a miraculous ordering principle, should not be present in the very texture of the world? Do not all phenomena arise from a manifestation of consciousness, awareness and power?

If the power hidden in the depths of matter does not arise from the universal intelligence, what factor guides it to the elaboration of forms, to an amazing regularity and harmony?

If that power is an agent devoid of intelligence and conscious will, why does it never fall prey to disorder, and why does its compounding of matter never result in collision and destruction?

It is here that belief in the creator bestows meaning on all existence and endows the world with sense and content. Those who possess deep vision and clear thought perceive plainly that an infinite power assures the preservation of the order of the world by means of firm supervision and absolute sovereignty.

In the past, everyone used to guide and control his own riding beast, and he was similarly accustomed throughout the ages to see an owner or supervisor in control of every piece of property, every scrap of land, every group or organization. Now matters are different. Today's man has gained access to remote-controlled satellites, electronic devices and pilotless planes, all equipped with automatic instruments and gadgets. Everyone knows that it is possible to construct a well-equipped machine that will react in appropriate ways to various contingencies, without the maker of the device being present or visible. We, therefore, no longer have the right obstinately to deny the existence of God simply because His hand is not visibly at work in the affairs of creation—visibly, that is, to our deficient understanding and knowledge.

It would, of course, be a highly defective analogy were we to draw a parallel with the maker of an artificial satellite or rocket who sitting in a fully equipped station on earth and with the aid of complex equipment guides and controls the course and movement of a spaceship. But if the intervention of God's hand in the order of creation is not visible to our physical eye and perception (although we can observe signs and indications that are like a ray proceeding from the splendor of His majesty) can we for that reason overlook the existence of a planner and mover who alone possesses true knowledge, power and will, simply because he cannot be contained in the narrow framework of time and space?

It is true that our capacities are limited in understanding a being who is without all like or exemplar in the sensory realm and whom human language is unable to describe fittingly and precisely. The lamp of our intelligence sheds little light on this endless plain, or—to put it differently—it encounters walls of limitation. At the same time, our relations in this world are with phenomena; that which impresses itself on our minds consists of the lines that are traced out by the observance of the objective world. But in perceiving that world, the problem of imagining it is removed from us; no barrier exists between our concepts and the necessary amount of cognition.

Nonetheless, certain skeptical persons who have abandoned the sound mode of thought that derives from man's essential nature and who have become limitingly accustomed to the existent entities of nature constantly await the occurrence of a miracle from God which will rupture the current order of nature in order to make a gift to them of faith and belief, making His existence readily comprehensible and acceptable.

However, they overlook that whatever new traces and signs of God might appear will cause only a temporary excitement and agitation; with the passage of time, they will become "normal" and no longer arouse attention.

Although all phenomena are now included in the framework of the order of creation, they began by rupturing the order of nature, and since all beings have been repeated on the stage of the world since the first manifestation, they now appear to be normal and customary.

By contrast, a sensorially imperceptible being—a being, moreover, that is replete with splendor and majesty and full of sanctity and greatness—will always influence men's souls. Their attention to such a being will, indeed, always increase and they will constantly look towards it with desire.

It is the dominance of a spirit of obstinacy, of judgment based on a discordant logic, that shackles human thought with limitations. For every creature in the order of being is an adequate proof for those who purse and empty their minds of obstinacy and the causes of denial.

Lesson Six
The Need of the World
for One Without Need

The principle of causality is a general and universal law and foundation for all efforts of man, both in the acquisition of knowledge and in his customary activities. The strivings of scholars to uncover the cause of every phenomenon, whether natural or social, arise from the belief that no phenomenon originates in and of itself without the intervention of causes and agents.

The researches of thinkers throughout the world have given them the ability to know better the powerful order of nature; the farther they advance on the path of knowledge, the more devoted they are to the principle of causality. The link between cause and effect and the principle that no phenomenon will set foot on the plain of being without a cause, are among the strongest deductions ever made by man and count as indispensable conditions for intellectual activity. They represent something natural and primordial, assimilated automatically by our minds.

Even prehistoric man was inclined to discover the causes of phenomena, and, in fact, philosophers derived the living concept of causality from the very nature and disposition of man before they placed it in a philosophical mould. Imprisoned as we are within the four walls of matter, we never encounter anything accidental in life, and, indeed, no one ever encountered, in the history of the world, an accident not arising from a cause. Were this not the case, we might have an excuse for regarding the universe as accidental in origin. What kind of accident might it be that from the dawn of being to the present has guided the infinite interactions of all things, in so wondrous, precise and orderly a fashion? Can the order we

perceive be the reflection of mere accident and happenstance?
*****

Any supposable phenomenon in the universe was submerged in the darkness of non-being before it assumed the form of being. It cannot pierce the darkness of non-being and step forth on the plain of being as an existent thing until the powerful hand of causality sets to work.

The relationship between cause and effect is the relationship between two existing things, in the sense that the existence of one of them is dependent on the existence of the other. Every effect has a relationship of affinity and harmony with its cause, since the effect draws its existence from the cause. This specific relationship cannot be destroyed or replaced by another.

Whenever you consider the quiddity of a thing that has an identical relationship to being and non-being, neither of them being rationally essential for it, that thing is technically designated as "contingent," in the sense that there is nothing within its essence necessitating either being or non-being. If a thing in its own essence requires its own non-being, then its existence is impossible. Finally, if being emerges from within the essence of a thing in such a way that reason cannot regard it as dependent on anything else, the existence of that thing is designated as necessary. It is an independent being, free of all need and subsisting by means of its own essence; its existence is the source of all other beings, while it is not subject itself to any need or condition.

It should be added that material existence cannot in any way acquire the attribute "necessary," because the existence of any compounded material entity is conditional on the existence of the parts that comprise it; it is dependent on its own parts both for its origin and for its survival.

Matter has different aspects and dimensions; it is immersed in quantity and multiplicity; and it acquires its various dimensions by means of attributes and properties. The necessary being, by contrast, is free of all such properties.
*****

All the phenomena that once did not exist and then came into being once possessed abstract notions of being and non-being. When they hastened toward the point of being, this was as a result of a cause that impelled them in that direction. It was an impulsion, an external factor, that drove them in one direction instead of the other. In other words, the existence of a cause was the agent of being, just as the non-existence or absence of a cause is the agent of non-being.

Of course, a phenomenon that comes into being as the result of the existence of a cause never loses its essential neediness; it will always remain a being characterized by need. For this reason, the need of a phenomenon for a cause is permanent and indissoluble; its relationship with the cause will never be severed for an instant. Were the relationship to be severed, the existence of the phenomenon would immediately yield to non-existence, in just the same way that the very instant an electricity generator stops working, all the bright lamps connected to it fall dark. It is for this reason that cause and effect, freedom from need and subjection to need, are in constant relationship with each other; were the relationship to be severed nothing would remain but darkness and non-being.

Thus, no phenomenon becomes manifest in the world until a certain power is bestowed on it by one whose essence is free from need and is itself the very source from which being gushes forth. Were being inherent in the essences of phenomena, they would never follow the path of cessation and non-being. But it is neediness that is inherent in their essences, so that even after their being is established in the order of creation, their attribute of neediness continues under all circumstances. They are never free of need for a cause; it is impossible that an effect should enjoy existence independently or continue to exist for a single instant without relying on a cause.

It thus becomes apparent to us that all phenomena—all contingent beings—derive at all times and in every instant from an infinite essence that bestows being—i.e., the Necessary Being, the Unique and Almighty Creator—the power and sustenance that permit them to come into being and remain in being.

The Noble Quran says: *"He it is Who from the plenitude of His essence has bestowed on us the capital of being."* (53:48) *"O mankind, you are in need of your Lord; it is only His unique essence that is free of need and worthy of praise."* (35:15)

Let us pay heed, too, to this Quranic summons: *"Do they imagine that they have been created without any cause, or do they suppose that they are their own creators?"* (52:36) *"Have they created the heavens and the earth? They have no certain belief in what they say."* (52:37) *"Do they have a Lord other than God? No, it is not so; God is exalted above the partners they ascribe to him."* (52:43) *"Glorified be He in Whose hand is all sovereignty and Who has power over all things."* (67:1)

The Source of All Being is Free of Need for a Cause

The followers of materialism pay much critical attention to the principle that God does not stand in need of a cause. They say if we suppose the Creator to be the origin of the world and the one who bestows existence upon it, all phenomena deriving their origination and continued existence from him, what cause has freed him of need for having a creator; what agent has caused him to come into being?

In a lecture given to the London Atheist Society, the well-known writer, Bertrand Russell, said: "One day, when I was eighteen years of age, I was reading the autobiography of John Stuart Mill. One sentence in particular caught my attention: Mill wrote that one day he asked his father who had brought him into existence, and his father had been unable to answer." The reason for this was that he immediately posed the question: who brought God into being?

Russell then adds: "I am still convinced that that simple sentence exposes the sophistry of the primary cause. For if everything must have a reason and cause, the same must apply to the existence of God. If, on the contrary, something can exist without reason or cause, that thing might be either God or the world, and the whole discussion becomes meaningless."[12]

Unfortunately, certain Western philosophers who accept the existence of God have been unable to solve this problem. The English philosopher Herbert Spencer has said the following in this connection: "The problem is that, on the one hand, human reason seeks a cause for everything and, on the other, refuses all circularity. It neither perceives nor comprehends an uncaused cause. When the priest tells a child that God has created the world, the child asks who has created God."[13]

Elsewhere he says: "The materialist tries to convince himself of a world that exists in and of itself, eternally and without cause. However, we cannot believe in something that has neither beginning nor cause. The theologian takes matters one step further back by saying that God created the world. But the child asks him the unanswerable question: who created God?"[14]

We can raise precisely the same objection against the materialists and ask them, "If we follow the chain of causality back, we will ultimately reach the primary cause. Let us say that cause is not God, but matter. Tell us who created primary matter. You who believe in the law of causality, answer us this: if matter is the ultimate cause of all things, what is the cause of matter? You say that the source of all phenomena is matter-energy; what is the cause and origin of matter-energy?"

Since the chain of causality cannot recede into infinity, they can answer only that matter is an eternal and timeless entity for which no beginning can be posited: matter is non-created, has no beginning or end, and its being arises from within its own nature.

This means that the materialists accept the principle of eternity and non-origination; they believe that all things arose out of eternal matter and that being arises from within the very nature of matter, without any need for a creator.

Russell openly states this belief in the lecture quoted above. He says: "There is no proof that the world ever had a beginning. The idea that things must once have had a beginning results from the poverty of our imagination."[15]

In just the same way that Russell regards matter as eternal, believers in God attribute eternity to God. Belief in an eternal being is then common to materialist and religious philosophers: both groups agree that there is a primary cause, but believers in God regard the primary cause as wise, all-knowing, and possessing the power of decision and will, whereas in the view of the materialists, the primary cause has neither consciousness, intelligence, perception, nor the power of decision. Thus, the removal of God in no way solves the problem posed by eternal being.

Moreover, matter is the locus for motion and change, and its motion is dynamic and situated within its own essence. Now, essential motion is incompatible with eternity, and matter and essential stability are two mutually exclusive categories that cannot be fused in a single locus. Whatever is stable and immutable in its essence cannot accept movement and change within that essence.

How do Marxists, who believe that matter is accompanied by its antithesis, justify the eternity of matter? Eternity means stability and immutability of essence, the impossibility of cessation, but matter is in its essence a compendium of forces and potentialities; it is relativity itself, totally caught up in living and dying.

Eternity is incompatible with the mode of being possessed by matter and the factors and attributes necessitated by its nature. The belief of those who have faith in God concerning a fixed and absolute principle relates to a being who in and of his nature can accept stability and absoluteness; his nature is completely devoid of and remote from the properties of matter. The very nature of matter refuses permanence, eternity and continuity, for it can never separate itself from movement, relativity, and it stands in opposition to being a prime or absolute agent.

It will be useful here to relate the discussion of Imam Sadiq, upon whom be peace, with one of the materialists of his age. The materialist: "Out of what were beings created?"

The Imam: "They were created out of nothing (i.e., they were originally non-beings)."

The materialist: "How do they grow and emerge from non-being?"

The Imam: "Did I not say that all things in the world were created out of nothing? My purport is this, that all beings were originally non-beings; they were non-existent, and then they became existent. You wish to say that the world is eternal, but this notion is incorrect for the following reasons:

"First, if the material world is eternal, it follows that an eternal being should be subject to change and cessation, which is impossible.

"Second, if the elements comprising the world are eternal by virtue of their essence, how is it possible that they should enter the embrace of death and disappearance? And if, conversely, they lack life in their essences, how can life surge forth from them?

"If you say that living beings emerge from living elements and inanimate beings from inanimate elements, we reply that an essence that lacks life in and of itself cannot be eternal and cannot be the source for life."

The materialist: "If matter is as you say, why are beings said to be eternal?"

The Imam: "Belief in the eternity of the universe is held by those who deny the existence of a ruler and planner of creation, reject the

messengers of God, regard the books they bring as the fables of the
ancients, and concoct beliefs pleasing to themselves."[16]

*****

We say, then, that the existence of a thing is not possible
without a cause of a deficient thing, that is, whose fate is in the
hands of its cause and whose permanence is dependent on the
existence of its cause. This does not apply to a being that is
conscious of its reality and exhibits no trace of defect and limitation.

The primary cause is the primary cause by virtue of possessing
perfect and unlimited being; not being subject to any agent, it is free
from need, condition and dependency, and it contains no trace of
mutability or change.

When we speak of the first cause and simultaneously assert
that God is free of all need for a cause, we do not mean that He
generally shares with created beings the need for a cause but was
once, as it were, granted an exemption from the law of causality.
God is not an effect in order that He might need a cause; He is not
a phenomenon in order that He might need a creator. On the
contrary, all manifestations and phenomena of being derive from
Him, the eternal source of being. The law of causality applies
uniquely to the sphere of those things whose non-existence preceded their existence.

Similarly, the meaning of the first cause is not that God originated Himself, that He was His own cause. The need of the effect
for the cause lies in the type of existence that the former possesses;
it exists not because it is essentially existent but as a result of the
derivative and dependent existence it acquires from the cause. But
a being whose nature is subject to no condition and exhibits a
complete absence of dependence and connection is totally removed
from the sphere in which the law of causality operates.

If a being, by virtue of the perfection and freedom from need of
its essence, stands in no need of a cause, it follows that no cause has
fixed it at a given degree of being and that no cause can intervene
in it.

The chain of causality cannot be extended indefinitely backwards, and an absence of connection is inherent in the very concept
of the first cause. The question, "Whence did the first cause arise?"
does not, therefore, arise; questions such as this apply only to the
origins of phenomena and their dependency.

The existence of the first cause is identical with its essence; its being the first cause is, indeed, also identical with its essence. Both these properties imply freedom from need, whereas things whose existence is borrowed stand in need of a cause, because they are characterized by transformation and change, by emergence from non-existence and entry into existence.

How can it be supposed that belief in the existence of God is the acceptance of contradiction, whereas belief in the uncaused nature of an effect such as matter is not contradictory?

We live in a world where all things are exposed to change and destruction; there is the mark of impermanence, subjection and indebtedness imprinted on each one of its particles. Need and dependence are firmly rooted in the depths of our being and that of everything on earth and in heaven. Our existence is not eternal and has not emerged from within our own essence; we were not, and then we were clothed in the garb of existence and came into being. In order to come into being, creatures such as us must beseechingly reach out to the bestower of existence.

But He Who is eternal and everlasting, Whose existence emerges from within His own essence, and Whose appearance is outside of time, manifestly has no need of a cause.

The meaning of a cause in philosophy is that which brings forth an effect from non-existence into existence and cloths it in the garb of existence. This creativity cannot be posited for material causes, and the only role of matter is to abandon one form in order to become receptive to another.

It is true that every material being acquires each instant a new and different character as a result of internal development. However, the innate motion of the world and the processes of generation and corruption proclaim a lasting need for a hand to that Who creates the motion, a hand that both nurtures the swift caravan of being and impels it forward.

Lesson Seven
The Finiteness of the Chain of Causality

The materialists may insist obstinately on denying the truth and put forward another specious argument. They may say, "We do not cut off the chain of causality but, on the contrary, perpetuate it indefinitely; we defend the principle of the infinite nature of the causative link."

In that case, they should be answered as follows: To analyze the world of creation in this manner rests on the supposition of a chain of causes and effects and the infinite unfolding of a succession of causes. However, since each cause is also an effect, it lacks being in its own essence; it is unable to partake of existence apart from the cause superior and precedent to it.

So how did each part of the chain, which is dominated by neediness from one end to another, emerge from non-being? The existence of each part of the chain manifests inadequacy, impotence, and origination in time; whence did its existence arise? How can great and complex beings emerge from infinite joinings of non-being? Does life gush forth from the union of the numerous factors that bring about death?

However far this infinite chain is prolonged, it will still have the attributes of neediness, dependency, and origination in time. A chain from the very nature of which autonomy and freedom from need do not arise can never put on the garment of being until it connects with one who is in his essence absolutely free of need— with a being who possesses the attributes of divinity and who is only a cause and not an effect. Without the existence of such an unconditional being, the source of all causes and the foundation of all existence, the order of creation cannot be explained.

Suppose that at the war front, a column of soldiers intends to attack the enemy but none of them is ready to begin the battle by lunging into the heart of the enemy army. Whoever is given the order to do so replies: "I will not attack until so-and-so beings to fight." Every single soldier repeats the same thing; there is no one unconditionally ready to begin the attack.

Under such conditions will the attack ever take place? Of course not, because everyone's fighting is conditional on that of someone else. It is obvious that a whole series of conditional attacks will not take place without the fulfillment of the condition, something impossible under the circumstances, and, as a result, the attack will not take place.

If we continue the chain of cause and effect indefinitely, the existence of each link in the chain will be conditional on that of the preceding link, which, in turn, will be conditional on the existence of the link preceding it. It is as if each link in the chain of causality were to proclaim loudly from the depths of its being: "I shall not don the garment of existence until that other one has set foot on the plain of being." Each link depends on a condition that has not been fulfilled, and each one is, therefore, barred from enjoying the blessing of existence.

Since we see the whole of the universe to be surging with different forms of being, there must exist in the world a cause that is not an effect, a condition that is not subject to a condition; otherwise the surface of the world would not be this thickly covered with phenomena.

That primary cause is one who, in his essence, is free of all need, who can dispense with all the different aspects of existence, and who is able to bring forth the most wondrous phenomena and the most original manifestations. He is a creator who plans all of this and then puts it into effect, who joins all of creation to a temporal mechanism, who constantly scatters the jewel of existence over the world, and who impels the great panorama of creation forward to fulfil the purposes of the order of being.

By making the world non-created and eternal, the materialists try to disprove the world's lasting need for a creator and thereby to bestow independent existence on the world. Their method, however, does not yield satisfactory results.

The materialist imagine that the world needs a creator only at the initial moment of creation; once the need is met, God and the world are independent of each other and have no links with each other. As a consequence of this belief, the materialist proceed to deny even that initial moment of need, and by rejecting the idea of a beginning for creation, they imagine they have solved the problem of God and creation and liberated the world of need for a creator.

This is because they imagine the need of the world to be temporary and passing, whereas the need is inherent in the essence of the world—the world is nothing but motion, a limited and dependent form of motion.

Each moment is, in fact, a beginning of creation; every instant, each atom in the world is engaged in origination. It follows that the whole of which the atoms are a part has similarly originated in time; it does not have an ipseity independent of that of the atoms composing it.

So the world still has the same need for a creator that it had at the moment when creation began. Even supposing the world to be eternal, it would still not enjoy autonomy of existence.

The Answer of Science to the Thesis of the Eternity of the World
Just as man gradually loses his faculties with the passage of time so that one day the lamp of his life is extinguished, so, too, the universe is constantly advancing toward collapse and dissolution. For the energies existing in the world are gradually becoming dulled; atoms become energy, and active energy becomes inactive and motionless. Once the atoms are uniformly and equally divided, nothing remains but absolute silence and immobility. It is, therefore, impossible to regard matter as the eternal essence or substance of being, and there is no choice but to regard the world as created.

The second principle of thermodynamics, entropy or the decline of thermal energy, teaches us that although we cannot fix a date for the appearance of the world, the world certainly did have a beginning. The heat in the world is gradually decreasing and falling, like a piece of molten iron that gradually diffuses its heat in the air until finally the heat of the iron will be identical with that of the objects and the air surrounding it.

If there were no beginning or point of departure for the world, all the existing atoms would have dissolved and been transformed into energy an infinite number of years ago. In the course of a very long past, the heat of the world would have come to an end, for matter, in the course of its successive and continuous transformation, is transformed into perishable energies. It is not possible for all the energy dispersed to be transformed anew into matter and mass comfortable to the world of being.

In accordance with the principle just mentioned, once usable energy is exhausted, chemical action and reaction can no longer take place. But given that chemical action and reaction do take place that life is possible on the earth, and that a huge body like the sun is divisible each day and night into three hundred thousand million tons, it is clear that the world has originated in time.

The death of planets and stars, the disappearance of suns, is a proof of death and mutation in the existing order; they show that the world is advancing towards non-being and an inevitable conclusion.

We see, then, that the natural sciences have expelled matter from the stronghold of eternity. Science not only proves the createdness of the world but also bears witness that the world came into existence at a given time.

The world at the time of its birth stood in need of a preternatural force, for at the beginning, all things were formless and undifferentiated. It was necessary for some primordial spark of motion and life to alight on the world of nature. How could an environment devoid of all active energy, characterized by absolute silence and formlessness, serve as the origin of motion and life?

Mechanics tells us that a motionless body is always motionless unless it becomes subject to a force external to itself. This law represents an inviolable principle in our material world, and we cannot, therefore, believe in a theory of probability or accident. Not a single motionless body has entered in motion up to now without being subject to an external force. So, based on this mechanical principle, a force must exist which being other than the world of matter, creates that world and imparts it with energy so that it takes shapes, differentiates itself, and acquires various aspects.

Frank Allen, an outstanding scientific personality, proposes the following interesting argument in favor of the creation of the world by God: "Many people have tried to demonstrate that the material world does not need a creator. What is above all doubt is that the world does exist, and four explanations can be proposed for its origin.

"The first is that despite what we have just said, we regard the world as a mere dream and illusion. The second is that it has emerged from non-being entirely of itself. The third is that the world did not have a beginning and that it has existed eternally. The fourth is that the world has been created.

"The first hypothesis depends on our accepting that there is, in reality, no problem to be solved apart from the metaphysical problem of man's awareness of self, which can also be dismissed as a dream, a fantasy, an illusion. It is possible that someone might say that imaginary railroad trains, full of imaginary passengers, are crossing non-existent rivers over immaterial bridges.

"The second hypothesis, that the world of matter and energy came into being entirely of itself, is as meaningless and absurd as the first; it is not even worth considering in discussing.

"The third hypothesis, that the world has always existed, has one element in common with the concept of creation, for either lifeless matter and the energy intermingled with it or a creator have always existed. Neither attribution of eternity presents any particular problem in itself. However, thermodynamics has proven that the world is advancing toward a state in which the heat of all bodies will be at a similarly low degree and usable energy will no longer be available. Life will then become impossible.

"If the world had no beginning and existed from all eternity, such a state of death and lifelessness would already have occurred. The brilliant warm sun, the stars and the earth full of life bear faithful witness to the world having originated in time; a particular moment in time marked the beginning of creation. The world, then, cannot be other than created; it must have been a supreme, primordial cause, an eternal, omniscient and omnipotent creator that brought the world into being."[17]

*****

If man thinks deeply a little and reflects on reality with broadness of vision, he will understand that faced with the vast geographic dimensions of existence and the need in some way to comprehend them, he can hardly regard his own capacity as adequate to the task. The knowledge of the system of creation accumulated by man through his untiring efforts is next to nothing. Although science has taken great steps forward, there is an utter disparity between man, what man has learned, and what he still does not know.

As far as those periods of the past are concerned that are shrouded in total darkness, for all we know, thousands or even millions of human species superior to the present one may have existed. Such species may yet come into being in the future.

What is called science by the science-worshippers of the present age and regarded by them as equivalent to the sum total of reality, is simply a collection of laws applicable to a single dimension of the world. The result of all human effort and experimentation is a body of knowledge concerning a minute bright dot— comparable to the dim light of a candle—surrounded by a dark night enveloping a huge desert of indefinite extent.

If we turn back millions of years, the dust of obscurity will cover our path as one emphatic indication of man's weakness and ignorance when confronted with the grandeur and vastness of nature.

It may be that the period in which man has existed is nothing more than an instant in the life of the world; it is certain that there was once a dark ocean of non-being in which there was no trace of man. In short, we know very little of the beginning of our journey and nothing of its future.

At the same time, it is impossible to believe that the conditions necessary for life exist exclusively on this tiny planet. Many scientists today regard the sphere of life as extremely vast and broad; they present countless millions of planets to our gaze and we look upon them by various means. But what we are thus enabled to see is nothing more than the field of vision of an ant when compared with the vastness of the universe.

Describing an imaginary journey to the world of infinity, Camille Flammarion, the famous scientist, says the following in his book on astronomy: "We continue to advance for a thousand years, for ten thousand years, for a hundred thousand years, at the same speed, steadily, without slowing down our vehicle, constantly moving forward along a straight line. We advance at a speed of three hundred thousand kilometers a second. Do we imagine that after travelling at that speed for a million years we will have reached the limits of the visible world?

"No, there are further dark, vast spaces that must be traversed, and there, too, new stars are visible at the limit of the heavens. We advance toward them, but will we ever reach them?

"More millions of years; more fresh discoveries; more splendor and grandeur; more new worlds and universes; more new beings and entities—will they never end? The horizon never closes; the heavens never bar our path; continual space, continual void. Where are we? What is the path we have followed? We are still in the middle of a dot—the center of the circle is everywhere, its circumference nowhere to be seen.

"Such is the infinite world that lies open before us, and the study of which has barely begun. We have seen nothing, and we turn back in fear, collapsing in exhaustion from this fruitless journey. But where are we to fall? We can fall for an eternity into unending whirlpools, the bottom of which we never reach, just as we cannot reach their summit. North becomes south; there is neither East nor West, neither up nor down, neither left nor right. In whatever direction we look, we see infinity, and within this endless expanse, our world is nothing more than a small island in a great archipelago spread out across an unending ocean. The entire life of humanity, for all the pride man takes in his political and religious history, or even the whole life of our planet with all of its splendor, is like the dream of a fleeting moment.

"If it were desired to write out again all the works of research penned by millions of scholars in millions of books, the ink required for the task would not exceed the capacity of a small tanker. But to describe and arrange in orderly fashion the forms of all existent things upon earth and in the heavens, in invisible past ages and in the infinite future—to write down, in short, all the mysteries of creation—might require more ink than the oceans contain water."[18]

As Professor Ravaillet says: "In order to have a complete conception of the world, it is enough to know that the number of galaxies in the infinite expanse of the universe is greater than that of all the grains of sand on all the shores in the world."[19]

Such considerations concerning what we know and what we do not know make it possible for us to escape imprisonment in the cocoon of our narrow life; to become humbly aware of how small we are; to go beyond this limited life of ours, to the degree that we are able; and to contemplate reality with greater care and profundity.

Lesson Eight
Pseudo-Scientific Demagoguery

The materialists claim that the establishment of their school of thought in the eighteenth and nineteenth centuries was directly connected to the progress of science and that the dialectical method was a fruit plucked from the fertile tree of science.

They depict every philosophy apart from materialism as a form of idealism, opposed to the scientific method of thought, and insist that their position is a scientific and progressive one. According to them, realism consists in turning away from metaphysical truths; everyone ought to base his worldview on sensory and empirical logic and opt for materialism. But this claim is nothing more than a fanatical illusion based on unproven theories. Views such as these derive directly from a system of thought centered on materialism; within it, everything is defined and delimited with reference to materialism.

Belief in an object of worship is without doubt one of the principal sources of human culture and knowledge. The propounding of belief in God as basis for a correct worldview has brought about profound changes in the foundations of society and thought throughout human history. Now, too, in the age of science and technology, when man has found his way into space, a considerable number of scientists have a religious outlook as part of the intellectual system; they have come to believe in the existence of a creator, a source for all beings, not only by means of the heart and the conscience, but also through deduction and logic.

*****

If the materialists' justification for their worldview were true, instead of being based on inadequate knowledge of the history of materialist thought, there ought to be a particular connection between science and an inclination to materialism; only materialist views would be represented in the realm of science.

Has every philosopher and scholar, in every age, held an atheistic worldview and belonged to the materialist camp? A scholarly examination of the lives and works of great thinkers will suffice to show that not only is the religious camp by no means empty of true scientists, but also that many great scientific thinkers and personalities, including the founders of much of contemporary science, have believed in monotheism.

In addition, materialistic and atheistic beliefs have by no means been confined to the period of the evolution and advancement of science; since ancient times and, indeed, throughout history, materialists have stood in opposition to a united front of believers.

Today it is primarily in a vulgarized form of Marxism that the wares of science have been turned into a tool of deception. Those who supposedly should be mapping out their path in the clear light of knowledge and weighing all matters with profound, logical perception and investigation, in complete freedom from all fanaticism and hasty prejudice—precisely these people have fallen prey to stagnation and blind imitation. They have arrogantly denied all values higher than intellect and reason, and even boast of their ignorant denial.

Their claim that the coming of science has put out the notion of God is purely rhetorical and has nothing to do with logical method, because even thousands of scientific experiments could not possibly suffice to demonstrate that no non-material being or factor exists.

Materialism is a metaphysical belief, and must, therefore, be proven or disproven according to philosophical method. Precisely for this reason, an acceptance of materialism cannot be made a basis for the denial of metaphysics. To interpret materialism in such a sense is in the final analysis strictly meaningless; it would be a superstitious notion involving the perversion of truth, and to regard it as scientific would, in fact, be treason to science.

It is true that until very recently man was largely unaware of the natural causes and factors that give rise to phenomena and that he had little awareness of the occurrences that took place around him. But his belief did not derive from ignorance, for if it did, the foundations of belief in God would have collapsed once certain facts concerning the world were discovered. On the contrary, we see in the present age that with the discovery of a whole mass of mysteries concerning creation, belief in God has taken on added dimensions.

Now science illumines a limited realm; the scientific worldview is a knowledge of the part, not a knowledge of the whole. Science is unable to demonstrate the aspect and form of the whole of creation. But at the same time, since the scientific mode of perception is precise and specific, belief in God acquires a more scientific nature and a new kind of logic through the advancement of science. Man's awareness comes into being through his perception of cause and effect, and one who believes in causality underlying phenomena cannot possibly ignore the role of the most fundamental factor that is at work over and above all other causes.

*****

Until very recently, man imagined his own being to consist simply of a symmetrical and well-proportioned form; he was unaware of the complex mysteries contained in his creation. Today he has discovered astounding and far-reaching truths concerning the interior of his slight being, realizing that there are tens of millions of billions of cells in the body. This makes possible a particular appreciation of the greatness of the creator responsible for this artifact that was not possible in the past.

Is it logical to say that belief in God is peculiar to those who know nothing about man's composition and creation, and that, by contrast, a scientist who is aware of the natural laws and factors responsible for man's growth and development, who knows that law and precise calculation preside over all stages of man's existence, is bound to believe that matter, lacking all perception and consciousness, is the source of the wondrous laws of nature?

Do scientific discoveries and knowledge cause such a scientist to conclude that matter, unknowing and unperceiving, is his creator and that of all beings? Materialism looks at the world with one eye closed and, as a result, is unable to answer numerous questions.

Science, too, offers no answer to the question of whether the world can be divided into two parts, material and non-material, or to the question of whether the world has an innate purpose. These questions do not belong to the realm of science; scientific knowledge can acquaint us—to a certain degree—with what is, but it is unable to show us a direction in life or inspire us with a path to be followed.

A scientific worldview cannot, then, be the foundation for a human ideology. The value of scientific knowledge is primarily practical, in that it enables man to dominate nature. It is ideal and theoretical values that are required as the foundation of belief.

Furthermore, science is based on experiment and investigation, and laws having experiment for their foundation are bound to be changing and unstable. Faith requires a basis that partakes of eternity, being immune against change, and is able to answer questions such as the nature and shape of the world as a whole in a trustworthy and permanent manner. Only thus can man's need for a comprehensive interpretation and analysis of existence be met.

As he advances toward perfection, man requires spiritual and intellectual equilibrium; lacking an aim, he will stray along false paths and risk disaster. A man who does not find his aim in religion will pursue an aim of his own making, which will be nothing other than a kind of revolt against the will of nature; it will have nothing to do with creativity or intellectual maturity.

The Reasons for Denial and Unbelief
Books on the history of religion try to delineate the factors that have drawn men to religion. But attempts such as they make are in vain and incapable of uncovering the truth of the matter. It is necessary to focus on man's innate tendency to monotheism, that primary existential characteristic of the human species which gives man—for all his internal contradictions, thoughts, and desires—a special place in creation. It then becomes possible to discover the factors that lead man to trample on his own nature by foreswearing religion.

Man's religious ties are an outgrowth of his nature, and materialism is something opposed to his nature. In accordance with his specific make-up, man will create his own god if he does not discover the true God, and the god he discovers may be nature or historical inevitability. This false god takes the place of the true God with respect to comprehensiveness of authority, effectiveness of decree, and capacity to guide man on a certain path and propel him forward, unhindered by anyone's desires.

This is the source of the trade in false gods, the adherence to the new idolatry, that would cruelly sacrifice God to history and exchange a pearl for a bead.

Alas that so many people smitten with self-inflicted abjection have bowed down before the idol they themselves have fashioned and deified! They have turned away from the peerless creator and willingly accepted the polluting disgrace of such misdirected worship.

If we examine the matter closely, we see that the appearance of materialism in Europe as a school of thought, the severance of men's links with a sublime principle, their imprisonment in the fetters of matter, the choice of science in place of religion—all this was caused by a series of social and historical factors that emerged in the West.

*****

One of the factors that aroused a widespread reaction in Europe and caused the emergence of freethinking and anti-religious propaganda, was the crushing pressure exerted by the Christian ecclesiastical authorities at the beginning of the Renaissance on scholars who were propounding new scientific ideas.

In addition to specifically religious doctrines, the Church was also beholden to certain scientific principles concerning man and the world that it had inherited from ancient—primarily Greek — philosophers and that it was placed on the same footing as religious beliefs. Whatever theory appeared to contradict the Bible and these inherited principles was regarded as heretical, and whoever espoused it would be severely punished.

The clear contradiction between science and religion created a mutual hostility in both camps. Intellectuals and scientists saw that the Christian church was enslaving intelligence and thought, preventing the free development of ideas; through its adherence to a petrified system of thought and an anti-intellectual tradition, it was creating a stifling atmosphere for the man of the new age. Thinkers thus retreated into a painful isolation from religion.

These accumulating pressures finally led to violent reactions that engulfed the whole of Europe. Once the power and dominion of the Church declined and its oppressiveness came to an end, Western thought recovered its lost freedom and reacted strongly against the limitations once imposed on it.

The intellectuals removed the chains of ancient ritual from their necks and turned away from religion. All the pain and anger they had felt found expression in a great wave of hostility to religion. An acute spiritual crisis began that culminated in the separation of science from religion. An illogical desire for vengeance on religion led to the denial of heavenly truths and of the existence of God.

It is true that some of the doctrines connected with religion were illogical or even baseless, having no connection with authentic religious knowledge. But to take revenge on the Church is one thing, and to fall into hasty and erroneous prejudice concerning religion, as such, is something else. It is obvious that vengeance, being a purely emotional matter, has nothing to do with scholarly precision.

The spiritual poverty of man thus advanced at a rate commensurate with his scientific and technological wealth. As he progressed in industry, he regressed in ethics and spirituality, to such a degree that he lacked the moral capacity to make proper use of his newly acquired knowledge.

Scientific knowledge is in itself indifferent to values; one cannot determine the duties of a responsible human being by referring to science. However far science advances, it cannot see more than one step ahead of itself. Human knowledge cannot attain to the essence of the world and perceive it in its totality, nor can it foretell the future destiny of man.

It is only the worldview of monotheism that does not attempt to confine man to the material aspects of his existence. On the contrary, through the symbols and signs that have been given to man to guide him on his path, monotheism delineates an exalted origin and destiny for man. Once man places himself on the path of monotheism, he acquires a comprehensive worldview within the framework of which he finds answers to his probing fundamental question. Once he has reached this stage of comprehensive and multidimensional belief, man's life takes on fresh vigor and the values that are the fruit of that worldview come to fruition. The struggle with the church was, then, one factor in the divorce of science from religion.

Another group abandoned religion and took refuge in materialism because the concepts propounded by the Church were improper and inadequate, lacking transcendental value. These concepts were naturally found unacceptable and unconvincing by intelligent people. The church would present God in material and human terms, in a sense that was opposed to the human desire for absolute values and the striving to break through and transcend all limiting frameworks.

There can be no doubt that if an indubitable truth is impressed in someone's mind in the defective form of a legend, that person will react negatively as soon as he reaches intellectual maturity.

Confronted with the anthropomorphic depiction of God made in Christian theology, the exaltation of belief over reason, and the insistence that faith should precede thought, enlightened people realized that these narrow-minded efforts to imprison wisdom and science in the monopoly held by Christian theology were incompatible with rational criteria and scientific method. Since they had no authentic source from which they might learn true teachings about God, being wholly dependent on the institutions of the Church and its corrupted books, and since they had no access to a superior system which would satisfy both their spiritual and their material needs and offer them a suitable framework for integrating all the vital elements of life, material and spiritual, emotional and intellectual, the worldview of materialism took root in them, leading to the denial of all transcendental and supra-human values.

They were unaware that although error leads religion astray when it follows the path of ignorance, true religion, free of all illusion, superstition and distortion, can liberate man from bondage to myth and superstition, hold him firm on the axis of true belief, and supply him with a correct understanding of teachings concerning God, one that satisfies the enquiring mind.

Instead, Western intellectuals were aware only of the superstitious aspect of false religion and how the established dogmas of religion lacked all logical basis, so they had no hesitation in condemning religion as such to be baseless. Their judgment was based on their discouraging experiences with their own religion, and it could not fail, then, to be hasty, unrealistic, irrational and illogical.

This is expressed as follows by a scholar of physiology and biochemistry: "The fact that certain scholars have not been led, in the course of their researches, to a perception of the existence of God, has numerous reason. Here we will mention only two of them. First, the political circumstances created by despotism, together with the attendant social and administrative conditions, have tended to cause men to deny the existence of the Maker. Second, human thought has always been influenced by certain fantasies and illusions, and although man may have no fear of spiritual or bodily torment, he is still not completely free to choose the right path.

"In Christian families, most children come to believe early in life in the existence of a God similar to man, as if man had been created in the form of God. When they begin to enter the realm of science and to learn and implement scientific concepts, they can no longer reconcile their feeble, anthropomorphic concept of God with the logical evidence and methods of science. So, after a certain time, when all hope of reconciling belief and science has disappeared, they totally abandon all concept of God and expel it from their minds.

"The main cause for this is that the evidence of logic and the categories of science do not modify their previous feelings and beliefs but, instead, cause them to feel that they were mistaken in their previous belief in God. Under the influence of this feeling, combined with other psychological factors, they are appalled at the inadequacy of their concepts and turn away from all attempts at the knowledge of God."[20]

Hence, scientists tried, by propounding all kinds of laws and formulae, to leave no place for God and religion in the solution of questions touching on existence and creation. They tried to sever men's hopes from religion and to depose God from playing any role in the functioning of the world and the ordering of nature.

Whenever they came to a dead end, they tried to solve the problem by means of various hypotheses or postpone its definite solution until more extensive research had taken place. They imagined that in this way they were avoiding surrender to non-scientific formulae and superstitions. Thus, although they did escape the perils of assigning polytheism, they regrettably took up arms for irreligion and atheism.

*****

Although a faith in God and belief in an originating principle is natural and innate in man, it cannot be compared to the material necessities of life which man constantly strives to obtain. It is quite distinct from material life, and being an inward need, belongs to a totally separate category.

In addition, it is easier to deny an invisible being than it is to affirm it, given our inability to describe it adequately. People who lack mental capacity, therefore, choose the easy and painless path of denial instead of undertaking mental exertion. The path of denial does not, moreover, involve any apparent harm. By turning away from God, people gradually acquire an attitude of obstinacy and hostility to religion, tainted with fanaticism. The profound effects of such an attitude can easily be seen in the malicious arguments of those who have turned their backs on religion.

It is also easier to deny an invisible being because to affirm it implies various obligations for man; those who wish to shake off those obligations simply deny the existence of an originating principle.

The Quran says: *"Does man wish to spend all the remaining days of his life in impiety and vain desire? For he asks, implying denial, 'When will be the day of resurrection and accounting?' Say: 'On a day when the eyes of mankind will be blinded in terror and fear."* (75:5-7)

*****

The teachings of ignorant and illogical professional ascetics also cannot be overlooked as a factor impelling certain groups of people in the direction of materialism.

The instincts that come into being together with the natural life of man that are intertwined with his existence, not only are not vain and purposeless; they are, also, a determining and destiny-shaping force, a factor of development and motion, that drives man forward to the purpose envisaged in his creation. It is true that man should not be a blindfolded slave to his instincts like a prisoner all of whose being and motions are under the control of the jailer. But he should also not do battle with the reality of his own being and seek to block all activity and movement on the part of his instincts. A fruitful existence for man is, in fact, dependent on the active presence in his life of his instincts, deployed in proper equilibrium; the suppression of the instincts leads to complexes and the destruction of the personality.

The worldview prevailing in Christianity during the Middle Ages was based on an exclusive orientation to the hereafter that entailed the devaluating of the material world. Now what will be the consequence if one denies all validity to the forces of instinct, in the name of God and religion, and even tries to annihilate them; if one sanctifies celibacy and monasticism and denounces as impure marriage and procreation, the very activity that secures the survival of the species; and if one regards poverty and deprivation as the guarantee of bliss? Will it, then, be possible to expect religion to play an active and creative role?

The true role and mission of religion is to refine, to guide and to control the instincts; to delimit the sphere of their activity; and to purge them of all perversion and excess. It is not to annihilate and abolish them.

Through controlling the instincts and striving always to free himself from the trap they may present, man creates a purposeful destiny for himself. If he fails to do this, the intense clash of instincts within him is so intense that he cannot easily be master of his own being. He, therefore, needs a comprehensive system of moral education.

Man is, on the one hand, subject to the influence of the religious impulse; this tames him inwardly and draws together his scattered energies in the grasp of its power, directing them toward the acquisition of virtue and benefit. On the other hand, he is also subject to the influence of his instincts.

In any society where people are constantly told, in the name of God and religion, that the path to happiness lies in turning one's back on the gifts of this world, an opening is automatically created for the development of materialism and a concentration on material values, so that the lofty concepts of religion, with all their far-reaching implications, disappear from the scene.

But this does not represent the true logic of religion. True religions direct man's attention to authentic spiritual values, basing themselves on belief in the creator and presenting man with comprehensive teachings and principles for living. They extend the field of his vision to the frontiers of the heavenly realm, deliver him from the servitude of self-worship and materialism, and, at the same time, permit him to enjoy material pleasures to a reasonable extent.

*****

Some people imagine that the free enjoyment of certain things religion has prohibited will guarantee them happiness. They think that religion is obstinately fighting against all enjoyment and is in no mood to compromise with the pleasures of this world, as if God were forcing man to choose between happiness in this world and happiness in the hereafter.

This attitude to religion is totally misleading and unrealistic. If religion seeks to play a role in man's efforts, and his choice of direction, it is because unbridled indulgence of desire, unconditional surrender to instinct and appetite, and obedience to the commands of the ego, darken man's life and propel him into a form of unconscious slavery. Despite his essentially pure nature, he falls from his true rank and strays from his real path. Were the free indulgence of instinctual desire not a cause of eternal misery and painful degradation, it would not have been forbidden.

It is considerations such as these which make it possible to understand why religion has forbidden certain things and how worldly happiness is compatible with happiness in the hereafter.

Similar considerations apply to the imposition on man of certain duties. The attempt to perform obligatory acts of worship, sincerely and without any hypocrisy, brings about an inward change in man; the purpose of these acts is not in any way to diminish man's worldly happiness.

Worship is like a tempest in the stagnant lagoon of the heart, transforming man's inner nature and his criteria of judgment. It is the cornerstone on which the foundation of religion is made firm, a fruitful educative practice that penetrates the depths of the soul. Its sharp sword severs the skein of corruption and lowliness in man, enabling him to take flight for a pure, vast and limitless realm. In short, it makes it possible for man to grow to true maturity.

Not only is there no contradiction between the concerns of life and those of the spirit; spiritual concerns are conducive to a life of greater happiness in this world.

It may be that the unconvincing and illogical teachings of Christianity have influenced the anti-religious tendencies of people like Bertrand Russell. He evidently believed that faith in God leads to unhappiness, as is apparent from the following words: "The teachings of the Church have made man choose between two forms of misery and deprivation: either misery in this world and deprivation of its enjoyments, or misery in the hereafter and deprivation of the joys of paradise. For the Church, one of these two forms of misery must necessarily be endured. One must either submit to misery in this world and suffer deprivation and isolation in order to enjoy pleasure in the hereafter, or, if one wishes to enjoy the pleasures of this world, he must accept that he will be deprived of pleasure in the hereafter."

The diffusion of opinions such as these, which display an intense and profound ignorance of the religious worldview, may determine the fate of the prevailing religion in a given society. Their effect on human beliefs and actions is too profound to be adequately measured with a passing, superficial glance. This mode of thought has caused the attention of man to be directed exclusively to the material sphere—consciously or unconsciously. The resulting concentration on pleasure and indulgence has caused the weakening of spiritual and moral concerns.

Religion does not condemn man to enduring one of two forms of misery. It is entirely possible to combine happiness in this world with happiness in the hereafter. Why should God, Whose treasury of mercy and grace is inexhaustible, not wish for His servants a complete happiness that embraces both this world and the hereafter? This is precisely what He does wish.

*****

Another factor in the spread of materialistic ideas has been indulgence of passion and immersion in the cesspool of lust. Every mental perception and idea forms the base of some external action; man's path of action takes shape under the influence of his beliefs. Conversely, man's actions and morals also bring about qualitative changes in his mental habits and mode of thought.

A man who worships his lusts will gradually lose all exalted ideas about God. Once he chooses an axis for his existence other than God and imagines that whatever exists in this world has simply been cast into it, free of any purpose, so that the very idea of an aim in life becomes meaningless, he begins to devote all his mental energies to the maximizing of pleasure. This humiliating plunge to a lowly plane of existence withers the roots of all aspiration for growth and development.

The idea of belief in God is, by contrast, like a seed that needs suitable soil in which to grow. It can blossom only in a pure environment, an environment in which man can swiftly and easily attain the degree of perfection that is peculiar to him, thanks to a framework in which the principles of his life are set down. Belief in God can never flourish in an unfavorable environment where corruption is rampant.

One of the obstacles to the knowledge of God and the reasons for man denying this existence, despite all the clear signs and decisive proofs that are available, is, then, surrender to sin and indulgence in passion.

Imam Ja'far as-Sadiq, upon whom be peace, said in answer to Mufaddal in the *Risalah-yi Ahlija*: "I swear by my own soul that God has not failed to make Himself known to the ignorant, for they see clear proofs and decisive indications of the Creator in His creation and behold wondrous phenomena in the kingdom of the heavens and on earth that point to their Creator.

"The ignorant are those who have opened the gates of sin before them and followed the path of indulgence in passion and lust. The desires of their souls have gained dominance over their hearts, and because of their oppression of their own selves, Satan has gained dominance over them. God has sealed the hearts of the transgressors."[20a]

The desire for comfort, contentiousness, profligacy, the weak logic of certain ignorant believers—these, too, are among the factors impelling men to materialism.

The chaos and confusion of life, the abundance of mass produced goods, affluence and power, the dazzling and distracting aspects of modern life, the proliferation of means for enjoyment and pleasure—all these completely overwhelm greedy men. They try completely to withdraw themselves from the sphere of religious concern and refuse to accept the authority of any superior power, for not only would this not bring them any material benefit, it would also rein in the tempest of their overweening desires.

In an environment where people are immersed in sin, dissipation and corruption, and refuse to accept any limitation governing their deeds, religion can exist only in name.

Self-indulgent and materialistic people cannot be seekers and worshippers of God. When one of the two opposing principles, pleasure-seeking and belief in God, has occupied the mental space of an individual, the other must necessarily vacate it. Once the spirit of worship prevails in human existence, it casts out all materialistic inclinations by severing the firm fetters of lowly desire and inspiring constant effort in man to ascend in the direction of his goal. Thus, a complete model of human freedom from slavery to nature emerges.

The more elevated and distant the goal man sets himself, the sharper is the incline leading toward it and the greater and more prolonged the effort required to reach it. So, if we choose God as our goal, we have chosen an infinitely elevated goal, and the path leading to attainment of the goal will be similarly infinite, although clear and straight at the same time. It is a goal that will answer many problems and questions, and since it will compel us to negate the tyranny of the ego, it will bestow absolute freedom on us.

If we accept God as our goal, freedom will be harmonized with our growth and development. Our efforts to develop and progress will take on content and meaning, thanks to the divine impulse and the desire for eternal life. In short, the desire for progress and advancement, once regulated by the worship of God, neither contradicts man's freedom nor results in his enslavement.

We can claim to have attained freedom only when we are in step with the universal advancement of the world toward perfection, deliberately, consciously, and in awareness of the benefits this will bring. To act in obedience to nature or historical inevitability is not freedom, for when man ignores his own welfare to follow the dictates of nature, this is nothing other than slavery or blind obedience.

Lesson Nine
How does the Quran present God?

When we wish to assess the scientific personality and knowledge of a scholar, we examine his works and subject them to close study. Similarly, in order to measure the talent, creativity and ability of an artist to invent original images, we undertake the study of his artistic production.

In the same way, we can also perceive the attributes and characteristics of the pure essence of the Creator from the qualities and orderliness that pervade all phenomena, together with their subtlety and precision. Thereby, within the limits set by our capacity to know and perceive, we can become acquainted with God's knowledge, wisdom, life and power.

If it be a question of complete and comprehensive knowledge of God, then, of course, we must accept that man's ability to know does not extent that far. God's characteristics cannot be placed within given limits, and whatever comparison or simile we offer for them is bound to be false, for whatever is observable to science and thought in the natural realm is the work of God and the product of His will and command, whereas His essence is not part of nature and does not belong to the category of created beings. Hence, the essence of the divine being cannot be grasped by man by way of comparison and analogy.

He is, in short, a being for the knowledge of Whose essence no measure or criterion exists and for the fixing of Whose power, authority and knowledge, we have no figures or statistics.

Is man, then, too abject and powerless to perceive anything of the essence and attributes of so elevated a reality? To concede the weakness of our powers and our inability to attain complete, profound and comprehensive knowledge of God does not imply that we are deprived of any form of knowledge, however relative.

The orderly pattern of the universe loudly proclaims His attributes to us, and we can deduce the power and unlimited creativity of the Lord from the beauty and value of nature. Phenomena are for us an indication of His unique essence.

Contemplation of the will, consciousness, knowledge and harmony inherent in the order of being and all the various phenomena of life, makes it possible for us to perceive that all these qualities—together with all the other elements that speak of aim, direction and purpose—necessarily derive from the will of a Creator Who Himself possesses these attributes before they are reflected in the mirror of creation.

That which comes to know God and to touch His being is the remarkable power of thought—a flash which deriving from that pre-eternal source shone on matter and bestowed on it the capacity of acquiring knowledge and advancing toward truth. It is within this great divine gift that the knowledge of God is manifested.

*****

Islam deals with the knowledge of God in a clear and novel way. The Quran, the fundamental source for learning the worldview of Islam, applies the method of negation and affirmation to this question.

First, it negated, by means of convincing proofs and indications, the existence of false gods, because in approaching the transcendent doctrine of unity, it is necessary first to negate all forms of pseudo-divinity and the worship of other-than-God. This is the first important step on the path to unity.

The Quran says: *"Have the ignorant polytheists abandoned the true God and chosen, instead, the false and powerless gods? Tell them: 'Bring forth your proof!' This call of mine to unity is my saying and that of all the learned men of the community, as well as the saying of all the Prophets and learned men before me. But these polytheists have no knowledge of the truth and constantly avert themselves from it."* (21:24)

"Say, O Messenger, 'You worship one other than God who has no power to help or to harm you. It is God Who is all-hearing and Who knows the state of all of creation.'" (5:79)

The one who has severed his connection with divine unity forgets, too, his own true position with respect to the world and being and becomes estranged from himself. For the ultimate form of self-alienation is the severing of all links with one's essential nature as man. Conversely, once man has become alienated from his own essence, under the influences of internal and external factors, he will also be separated from his God and become en- slaved by other-than-God. Subordination to other-than-God, then, takes the place of all logical thought. This represents a reversion to the worship of phenomena, for worshipping an idol and according primacy to matter both are forms of regression that rob man of his innate capacity for growth.

Monotheism is the only force that makes it possible for man to recapture the creativity of human values. By regaining his true rank, he enters a state of harmony with his own human nature and the ultimate nature of all being, thus attaining the most perfect form of existence open to him.

Throughout history, all divine summons and movements have begun with the proclamation of divine unity and the exclusive lordship of God. No concept has ever occurred to man that is more productive of creative insights and more relevant to the various dimensions of human existence, or a more effective brake on human perversity, than the concept of divine unity.

Using clear proofs, the Quran shows man the way to attaining knowledge of the divine essence as follows: *"Did man emerge from non-being through his own devices? Was he his own creator? Did mankind create the heavens and earth? Certainly they do not know God."* (52:35-36)

The Quran leaves it to man's reason and commonsense to realize the falsity of these two hypotheses—that man came into being of himself, or that he was his own creator—by testing and analyzing them in the laboratory of his thought. By reflecting on the signs and indications of God, he will come to recognize with clear and absolute certainty the true source of all being and to under- stand that no value can be posited for any model of the universe unless behind it an organizing and capable intellect is at work.

In other verses, man's attention is drawn to the manner of his creation and gradual emergence from non-being. He, thus, comes to realize that his remarkable creation, with all the wonders it contains, is a sign and indication of the infinite divine will, the penetrating rays of which touch all beings.

The Quran says: *"We created man out of an essence of clay, then We established him in a firm place in the form of sperm. Then We made the sperm into coagulated blood, and then into a formless lump of flesh. Then we made it into bones, and then clothed the bones with flesh. Finally We brought forth a new creation. How well did God create, the best of all creators!"* (23:12-14)

When the foetus is ready to receive shape and form, all the cells of the eyes, the ear, the brain, and the other organs, start to function and begin their ceaseless activity. This is the truth to which the Quran is directing men's attention. It, then, poses to man the question of whether all these wondrous changes are rationally compatible with the hypothesis that there is no God.

Is it not rather the case that phenomena such as these prove and demonstrate, with the utmost emphasis, the need for a plan, a design, a guiding hand inspired by conscious will? Is it at all possible that the cells of the body should learn their functions, pursue their aim in a precise and orderly fashion, and crystallize so miraculously in the world of being, without there being a conscious and powerful being to instruct them?

The Quran answers this question as follows: *"He it is Who creates and brings forth (the totality of parts), Who separates (the parts belonging to each organ), and Who gives form (to different aspects)."* (59:24)

The Quran describes every sense phenomenon that man sees around him as something calling for reflection and the drawing of conclusions. *"Your God is but one God. There is no god other than Him, Compassionate and Merciful. In the creation of the heavens and the earth, in the alternation of night and day, in the ships that ply the seas to the benefit of man, in the water sent down from the heavens to revive the earth after its death, in the different species of animals scattered across the earth, in the rotation of the winds, in the clouds that are subordinate to God's command between heaven and earth—in all of this, there are signs for men who use their intellects."* (2:163-164) *"Tell men to reflect with care and see what things the heavens and the earth contain."* (10:101)

The Quran also mentions the study of human history and the peoples of the past with all the changes they have undergone, as a special source of knowledge. It invites man to pay heed, in order to discover the truth, to the triumphs and defeats, the glories and humiliations, the fortune and misfortune, of various ancient peoples, so that by learning the orderly and precise laws of history, he will be able to benefit himself and his society by aligning the history of his own age with those laws.

The Quran thus proclaims: *"Even before your time, certain laws and norms were in force, so travel and examine the historical traces left by past peoples, to see what was the fate of those who denied the truths of revelation and the promises of God."* (3:137) *"How many were those powerful ones whom We destroyed in their cities on account of their oppression and wrongdoing, and We made another people to be their heirs."* (21:11)

The Quran also recognizes man's inner world, which it expressed by the word *anfus* ("souls"), as a source for fruitful reflection and the discovery of truth. It points out its importance as follows: *"We make our signs and indications entirely manifest in the world and in the souls and inner beings of Our servants so that it should be clear that God is the True."* (41:53) *"On the face of the earth there are signs for the possessors of certainty, and also in your own selves; will you not see?"* (51:20-21)

In other words, there is an abundant source of knowledge in the beauty and symmetry of the human body, with all of its organs and capacities, its actions and reactions, its precise and subtle mechanisms, its varied energies and instincts, its perceptions, feelings and sensations, both animal and human, and most especially in the astounding capacity of thought and awareness with which man has been entrusted—a capacity which still remains largely unknown, for man has taken only a few steps in studying this invisible power and its relationship with his material body.

The Quran proclaims that it is sufficient to reflect on and examine your own self in order to be guided to the eternal, infinite source that is free of all need, has unlimited knowledge, skill and power, and a feeble reflection of which is manifest in your being. You will then know that it is that infinite reality which has thus brought together in one place so fruitful a compound of elements and brought it forth onto the plain of existence.

Given the existence of such vivid indications and decisive proofs, placed at your disposal and within your own being for you to seek the knowledge of God, no excuse will be accepted from you for misguidance and denial.

The Quran also applies the method of negation and affirmation to the question of God's attributes. Thus, it describes the attributes that the essence of the Creator possesses as "affirmative attributes." Among them are knowledge, power, will, the fact that His existence was not preceded by non-existence and that His being has no beginning, and the fact that all the motions of the world derive from His will and His power.

The Quran says: *"He is God, the One other than Whom there is no god, the knower of the hidden and the manifest, the Compassionate, the Merciful. He is God, the One other than Whom there is no god, the Commander, the All-powerful, Pure and Without Defect, the Bestower of Safety, the Protector, the Precious, the Mighty, the Sublime, the Most Elevated. Exempt and purified be He from the partners which they ascribe to Him."* (59:22-23)

The "negative attributes" are those from which God is free. They include the fact that God is not a body and has no place; His sacred being has no partner or like; He is not a prisoner to the limitations set up by the bounds of the senses; He neither begets nor is begotten; there is neither change nor motion within His essence, for He is absolute perfection; and He does not delegate the task of creation to anyone.

The Quran says: *"O Messenger, say: 'He is God, the One, the God Who is free of need for all things and of Whom all beings stand in need. No one is His offspring, and He is not the offspring of anyone, and He has no like or parallel.'"* (112:1-4) *"Pure and exalted is thy Lord, God the Powerful and Unique, Who is pure of what men in their ignorance ascribe to Him."* (37:180)

Human logic, which inevitably thinks in terms of limited categories, is incapable of sitting in judgment on divinity, because we must admit that it is impossible to perceive the ultimate ground of that being for whom no observable or comprehensible analogue or parallel exists in the world of creation. The most profound schools of thought and the greatest methods of reflection here fall prey to bewilderment.

Just as all existent beings must lead back to an essence with which existence is identical, to an independent being on which all other beings depend, so, too, they must derive from a source of life, power and knowledge, from the infinite being of which all these attributes and qualities surge forth in abundance.

Lesson Ten
The Conditions for an Ideal Object of Worship

The Lord of the World, as presented in the Quran, possesses all the necessary conditions of an ideal object of worship. He is the creator of love and all forms of beauty, the originator of all forms of power and energy. He is a vast ocean on the slightest ripple of whose surface the swimmer of the intellect is tossed around like a plaything. It is He Who preserves the heavens from falling and the earth from collapsing. If, for an instant, He closes His eye of mercy or averts it from this world, the whole of the universe will perish and hurtle toward non-being in the form of dust. The existence and survival of every atom in the universe is, therefore, dependent on Him.

It is He Who bestows all bounties and all felicities, Who owns us and may freely dispose of us. When He commands and an order goes forth, as soon as He says, *"Be!,"* a creature comes into being.

Truth and reality derive their substance from His essence, and freedom, justice, and other virtues and perfections derive from the rays of His attributes. To take flight towards Him, seek to draw near to His glorious threshold, is to attain all conceivable desire at the highest degree. Whoever gives his heart to God, gains an affectionate companion and a loving friend; the one who relies upon Him has placed his hope on a firm foundation, while the one who attaches his heart to other-than-God is a prey to illusion and builds a foundation on wind.

He Who is aware of the slightest motion that takes place anywhere in creation can also determine for us a path leading to happiness and lay down a way of life and a system of human relations that conforms to the norms He has established in the order of creation. He is, after all, aware of our true interests, and it is even

His right alone to lay down a path for us as the logical outcome and natural consequence of His divinity. To act in accordance with the program He lays down is the only certain guarantee for our ascent toward Him.

How is it possible that man should be so enamored of truth and justice that he is ready to sacrifice his life for their sake, unless he is aware of their source and origin?

If a being is worthy of worship, it cannot be anyone other than the Creator Who is the axis of all being. No thing and no person has such a rank as to deserve the praise and service of man. All values other than God lack absoluteness and primacy and do not subsist in and of themselves; they are relative and serve only as a means for the attainment of degrees higher than themselves.

The primary qualities that elicit man's worship are being the bestower of all bounties and being aware of all the possibilities, needs, capacities and energies contained in man's body and soul. These qualities belong exclusively to God; all beings stand in need of and rely upon that being Who is existent by by virtue of His own essence. The caravan of existence is constantly moving toward Him by means of His aid, and His commands descend unceasingly of every speck in the universe.

Absolute submission and worship belong, then, exclusively to His Most Sacred Essence. His glorious presence, uninterrupted by a single moment of absence, is felt at the heart of each atom of being. All things other than God resemble us in that impotence and deficiency prevail over them. They are, therefore, unworthy of our submission and are not worthy of usurping sovereignty over any part of God's realm, which is the whole broad plain of existence. Man, too, is too noble and valuable a being to be subjected and humbled by anything other than God.

In the whole broad plain of being, it is God alone Who deserves man's praise. Man must grant to his love of God, to his efforts to draw near to Him and earn His pleasure, precedence over all other beings and objects of love. This will result in the ennobling of man and, the augmenting of his value, for man is but a small drop and if not united with the ocean, he will be swept away by the storm of corruption, dried up by the burning sun of chaos. Man gains his true personality and becomes eternal when he attaches himself to that effulgent source, when God gives meaning to his world and becomes the interpreter of all the events of his life. It is in this sense that men's worlds may be either broad and expansive or narrow and constricting.

The Commander of the Faithful, Ali, peace be upon him, says, in discussing the weaknesses of man and his limited capacities: "How strange and remarkable is the affair of man! If he becomes hopeful with regard to a certain desire, greed will render him abject; desire will lead to greed, and greed will destroy him. If he falls prey to hopelessness, grief and sorrow will kill him. If he attains happiness and good fortune, he will fail to preserve them. If he falls prey to terror and fear, they will reduce him to utter confusion. If abundant safety is granted him, he will become negligent. If his blessings are restored to him, he will become arrogant and rebellious. If he is stricken with misfortune, sorrow and grief will disgrace him. If he acquires wealth, he will become overweening. If poverty lays hold of him, he will be plunged in misery. If he is weakened by hunger, he will be unable to rise from the ground. If he eats to excess, the pressure of his stomach will discomfort him. So all deficiency in the life of man is harmful, and all excess leads to corruption and ruin."[21]

Generally speaking, justice, nobility, virtue and other qualities that earn respect and praise must either be illusionary and imaginary, or we must consider these values as real and necessary, based on the perceptions of conscience and instinct. In the latter case, we ought humbly to submit to that universal existence and absolute perfection which flows over with virtue, life and power, and from which all values derive.

*****

When we look into the matter carefully, we see that all the countless beings that exist in the world, as well as the love and aspirations that are rooted in the depths of our being, all converge at one point, all revert to one source—God. The very essence and reality of the world is identical with its connection, relation and attachment to God. Being reascends by a different route to the point where it began and from which it descended, and that point alone is worthy of man's love and devotion. Once man discovers this point, he becomes so enamored of its absolute beauty and perfection that he forgets all else.

We see that all phenomena have emerged from non-being into

a state of being, and that throughout the period of their existence, whether short or long, they are dependent on a source external to themselves for aid and sustenance; they are marked indelibly with subordination and lack of autonomy.

If the ideal object of worship we seek and toward which we are attempting to advance were unaware of the pains we suffer and the nature of the world; if it were unable to satisfy our desires and longings, being replete with impotence and deficiency just like ourselves and belonging to the same category as us—it could not possibly be our final aim and ultimate object or possess absolute value.

When we seek the fulfillment of a wish by means of our worship, it is God alone Who can respond by meeting our needs. The Quran says: "*Those whom you call upon other than God are servants like yourselves (i.e., they have no power of themselves)*." (7:194)

The Commander of the Faithful, upon whom be peace, while supplicating his Lord in the mosque of Kufa, said: "O my Master, O my Master! You are God the Great and I am your wretched and insignificant slave. Who can show mercy to His insignificant slave but God the Great? O Master of mine, O Master of mine! You are strong and powerful, I am weak and impotent; other than one strong and powerful, who can show mercy to the weak?

"O Master of mine, O Master of mine! You it is Who bestows generosity on the beggar, and I stand as a beggar at your threshold. Who will show mercy to the beggar other than the generous and the munificent one?

"O Master of mine, O master of mine! You are eternal existence and I am a creature destined to perish. Who will have mercy on one destined to perish other than the eternal, everlasting essence?

"O Master of mine, O Master of mine! You are the guide Who points out the way, and I am lost and bewildered. Who will take pity on the lost and bewildered if not the guide Who points out the way?

"O Master of mine, O Master of mine! Have mercy upon me by Your infinite mercy; accept and be satisfied with me in Your generosity, favor and kindness, O God, possessor of generosity, favor and kindness, and in Your all-embracing mercy, O most merciful of the merciful!"[22]

Thus, to show reverence to other-than-God, to orient oneself to other than His pure essence, is in no way justifiable; apart from God, nothing can have the slightest effect on our true destiny. If an object of worship deserves man's devotion and love and is capable of lifting him to the peaks of felicity, that object of worship must be free of all deficiency and inadequacy. Its eternal rays must touch all creatures with sustenance and life, and its beauty must cause every possessor of insight to kneel down in front of it. Possessing infinite power, it quenches the burning thirst of our spirits, and gaining knowledge of it, is nothing other than attaining the ultimate source of our true nature.

If we choose an object of love and worship other than God, it may have certain capacities and be able to fulfill our desires up to a point, but once we reach that point, it will no longer be an object of love and worship for us. It will no longer be able to arouse and attract us; it will, on the contrary, cause us to stagnate. For not only will it not satisfy our instinctive desire to worship, it will prevent us from reflecting on any higher value and imprison us in a narrow circle, in such a way that we no longer have any motive to advance or ascend.

If the object we choose to worship and love be inferior to us, it can never cause us to ascend and refine our beings. Our inclination to it will, on the contrary, drag us down to decline, and we will, then, be like the needle of a compass which is diverted from the pole under the influence of a completely alien magnetic field. The result will be total loss of direction; eternal misery will become man's inevitable destiny.

Worship, Man's Loftiest of Expression of Gratitude

An object of worship can give direction to man's motion and light up his darkness with its brightness when it is able to give him ideals, is endowed with a positive and elevated existence, is the cause of effects, and is the very essence of stability and permanence. Then, the object of worship produces inner effects in man and guides him in his thought and his actions. It facilitates for the essence of man, that part of him nurtured by the divine wisdom, its search for perfection.

Any effort or motion on the part of man to choose a false direction for himself, to take the wrong path in life, will result in his alienation from himself, his loss of all content, and the distortion of his personality. Man cannot possibly come to know himself correctly if he has separated himself from his Creator. To forget God means to forget oneself, to be oblivious to the universal purposes of human life and the world that surrounds one, and to be unable to reflect on any form of higher values.

Just as attachment to other-than-God alienates man from himself and transforms him into a kind of moving biological machine, so, too, does reliance on God and supplication at His threshold draw mono-dimensional man, lacking all spiritual life, up from the oceanic depths of neglect, revive him and restore him to himself.

Through worshipping God, the spiritual capacities and celestial forces in man are nourished. Man comes to understand the lowliness of his worthless material, hopes and desires and to see the deficiencies and weaknesses without his own being. In short, he comes to see himself as he is.

To be aware of God and take flight toward the invisible source of all being illumines and vivifies the heart. It is utterly pleasurable, a pleasure that cannot be compared to the pleasures of the three-dimensional material world. It is through orienting oneself to that abstract, non-material reality that thoughts become lofty and values transformed.

The Commander of the Faithful, Ali, peace be upon him, discusses the wonderful effect of awareness of God on men's hearts as follows: "The Almighty Creator has made awareness of Him the means for purifying the heart. It is through the awareness of God that deaf hearts begin to hear, blind hearts begin to see, and rebellious hearts become soft and tractable."[23]

He says, too: "O Lord! You are the best companion for those who love You and the best source of remedy for all who place reliance upon You. You observe them in their inner states and outer doings and are aware of the depths of their hearts. You know the extent of their insight and knowledge, and their secrets are manifest to You. Their hearts tremble in separation from You, and if solitude causes them fear and unease, the awareness of You comforts them, and if hardship and difficulty assail them, You alone are their refuge."[24]

Imam Sajjad, upon whom be peace, that paragon of purity and justice who had an unbreakable bond with his Lord, demonstrates to us in his supplicatory prayers the highest expression of love.

This was a sacred love that had inflamed all of his being, and although his spirit was sorely pressed by the mortal sorrow of separation, the powerful wing of love enabled him to soar up into the limitless heavens. With indescribable sincerity and humility, he thus prayed at the threshold of God, the Eternal: "O Lord! I have migrated to Your forgiveness and set out to Your mercy. I ardently desire Your pardon and rely on Your generosity, for there is naught in my conduct to make me worthy of forgiveness, and Your kindness is my only hope.

"O God, send me forth on the best path and grant that I die as a believer in Your religion and be resurrected as a believer in Your religion.

"O Lord Whom I worship! O You whose aid the sinners supplicate through Your mercy! O you in the remembrance of Whose generosity the wretched seek refuge! O You in fear of whom the wrongdoers bitterly weep!

"O source of tranquility for the heart of those banished in fear from their homes! O consoler of those who sorrow with broken hearts! O succorer of the lonely, helper of the rejected and needy! I am that servant who responded obediently when You commanded men to call on you.

"O Lord! Here I am prostrate in the dust at Your threshold. O God, if You show mercy to whomever calls upon You in supplication, then let me be earnest in my supplications, or if You forgive whomever weeps in Your presence, then let me hasten to weep.

"O God, do not make hopeless the one who finds no giver but You; do not thrust me away with the hand of rejection now that I stand here at Your threshold." [25]

Anyone who wishes to understand the profound meaning of supplication must realize that rational explanation and logical deduction are incapable of yielding a deep understanding of questions touching on spiritual illumination.

The Noble Quran describes the conduct and way of life of the unbelievers and materialists as follows: *"The deeds of those who are unbelievers are like a mirage in a flat and waterless desert. A thirsty man will imagine them to be water and hasten toward them, but when he reaches them, he will find no water."* (24:39)

"God and His Messengers summon mankind to the truth; other than God, all claims are baseless and vain, for they are unable to meet any of

man's needs. One who relies upon them will be like the one who dipped his hand in a well to drink from it but found his hand could not reach the water. The unbelievers summon men only to misguidance." (13:14) *"The dwelling of those who choose other than God as friends and protectors is like the dwelling of the spider; were the spider to know, the weakest of dwellings is his."* (29:41) *"The deeds of those who disbelieve in God are like ashes that are swept away by a strong wind; they have no benefit from all their strivings. This is the path of misguidance, utterly distinct from the path of salvation."* (14:18)

The loftiest expression of thankfulness that man can make at the threshold of his true object of worship is supplication, the profession of love for His absolute perfection and devotion to it. This he does in harmony with all of creation, because all beings praise and glorify God.

The Quran says: *"The seven heavens and the earth and all they contain praise God. There is no creature not engaged in the praise and magnification of its Lord, but you do not understand their praise. God Almighty is forbearing and most forgiving."* (17:44)

This worship and praise naturally do not bring God the slightest benefit, for He possesses all perfections to an infinite degree and neither the world nor man can add anything to Him or take anything away from Him. Is it at all conceivable that He would create man in order to benefit from his worship and praise? On the contrary, it is man who, by gaining knowledge of the supreme being and worshipping Him in His sublimity, reaches his ultimate aim and true perfection.

Professor Ravaillet, celebrated philosopher and physicist, has the following to say about consciousness in the universe: "The new cosmology says that atoms and molecules know what they are doing; in the normal sense of the word, they have awareness of the tasks they perform and of the course of their lives. This consciousness of theirs is superior to the knowledge of the physicist, because all the physicist knows of an atom is that if it were not tangible and recognizable, no one would know anything about it.

"Bodies, motion, speed, the concepts of here and there, radiation, equilibrium, space, atmosphere, distance, together with many other things—all came into existence thanks to the atom. If the atom were not to exist, what would be the origin of all the remarkable phenomena of creation? There exists the same affinity between consciousness and body as there does between motion and motion-lessness, or the positive and negative aspects of motion.

"Now, space, taken as a whole, is not blind. We demonstrated, if you remember, when examining the field of vision, that the eye is not the basic and determining factor. Since it is fixed at a given point on the globe, according to the limited circumstances of the human species and other terrestrial beings, it has a certain narrow physical field within which it operates. But as for the space between the earth and the sun, between the sun and the galaxies, and between the galaxies and remote gigantic planets, where huge forces with tremendous range are engaged in exchanging energy—there an organ such as the eye of terrestrial creatures has no opportunity to show itself or demonstrate its effectiveness.

"But precisely for this reason we cannot believe that lack of consciousness and awareness prevail in that field for the exchange of vast energies and forces ruled by the laws of attraction, equilibrium, motion, light and centrifugal force. Blindness does not exist in these wondrous phenomena, and even particles of light cannot be regarded as something akin to an illiterate mailman whose only job is to deliver messages he cannot read."[26]

Lesson Eleven
The Incomparability
of the Divine Attributes

In our efforts to describe the Creator and gain knowledge of His attributes, we ideally need concepts and expressions that are beyond our reach. Those terms we do employ are unable to help us in reaching our goal, a true description of God, for our limited understandings cannot accommodate a perception of the nature of God's infinite attributes. He is exalted above all concepts coined and fashioned by the human mind.

Man, who is created and limited in every respect, should not expect to be able to assess and describe a non-material being by means of material attributes and characteristics.

A reality that is other than contingent beings and natural beings, whose absolute power and infinite knowledge encompass all things, who in the words of the Quran, *"has no similarity to finite and deficient created beings,"* (42:11) such a reality naturally cannot be discussed in the same breath as ordinary topics.

Ali, upon whom be peace, the Master of the God-fearing, said: "Whoever compares and assimilates God to something or refers to His sacred essence, has not, in reality, had Him in view. Whatever man knows to be the ground of His essence must necessarily be created. God is the Creator and Maker. Whatever depends on other than itself is caused and created. It is God alone who is only a cause (and not an effect).

"He undertakes creation without any means of instruments. He measures without having recourse to thought and reflection. He is free of all need and derives no profit from anything. Time and place do not accompany Him. Tools and instruments do not aid Him. His existence precedes all time and His pre-eternity precedes all beginning.

"He is not limited by any limit, for it is phenomena that delimit their essence by means of the limits peculiar to them and it is bodies that indicate their likes. His sacred essence does not admit the concepts of motion and motionlessness; how is it possible that something created within phenomena should also exist in His being?

"Were there to be motion and stillness in His essence, He would be exposed to mutation and change; He would be divisible and the pre-eternity of His being would be negated.

"He is the source of all powers, and hence no being can have any effect upon Him. Finally, He is the Creator Who does not change or disappear and Who is never hidden from the people of knowledge and insight."[27]

The fact that God's attributes are utterly separate from ours and cannot be examined through a comparison with our attributes is because the attributes of that fountainhead of being are different from the attributes of all other beings.

For example, we have the ability to perform certain tasks, but this is not the same as the power of God; in our case, the attribute is one thing and the entity it describes is another. When we boast of our knowledge, we are not one and identical with our knowledge. During infancy there was no trace of learning or knowledge in our beings, but later we gradually acquired a certain amount of knowledge by learning. Knowledge and power form two distinct corners of our being; they are neither identical with our essence nor are they united with each other in our being. The attributes are accidents and our essence is a substance; each is independent of the other.

But the case of the divine attributes is fundamentally different. When we say that God is all-knowing and all-powerful, what we mean is that He is the source of knowledge and power: the attribute is not something other than the entity it describes although it is conceptually distinct. In reality, His attributes are identical with His essence; for His essence does not constitute a substance to which accidents might adhere. He is absolute being, identical with knowledge, power, life, stability and realization; He is not subject to any mental or external limit or restriction.

Since we are nurtured in the very heart of nature and are, therefore, familiar with it at all times, and since whatever we see has particular dimensions and shape, a time and a place, and all the other properties of bodies—in short, because of the habituation of our mind to natural phenomena—we try to measure all things with the criteria of nature, even intellectual and rational concepts. The criteria of nature thus serve as the point of departure for all scientific and philosophical investigations.

To imagine a being who has none of the properties of matter and who is other than whatever our minds might conceive, and to understand attributes that are inseparable from the essence, not only requires great precision but also demands of us that we completely empty our mind of material beings.

Ali, peace be upon him, has spoken eloquently, profoundly and meaningfully on this matter. He emphasizes that men cannot imprison God in a description, saying: "Pure monotheism and perfect faith lie in exempting, negating and excluding from His sacred essence all the attributes of created beings. God forbid that He should be described by any such attribute, because when He is so described, it appears as if each attribute is separate from its possessor and alien to it. So one who says something in description of the Creator imagining Him to possess some attribute superadded to the essence has made Him the partner of something and suggested He consists of two parts. Such an attempt to describe God arises from ignorance and lack of awareness."[28]

Mental concepts cannot describe God by recourse to finite attributes; being limited, they are inapplicable to God's being. Each attribute, with respect to the particular meaning it conveys, is separate from all other attributes. For example, the attribute of life is quite different from the attribute of power; they are not interchangeable. It is possible that certain instances might gather all these attributes together in a single location, but each of them lexically has a different purport.

When the human mind wishes to ascribe an attribute to a certain thing, his aim is to establish in a given instance a kind of unity between the attribute and the entity it describes. But since the attribute is conceptually distinct from the entity, the mind inevitably decrees that they remain separate from each other. The only means for the knowledge of things is to describe them through the use of mental concepts, which are conceptually separate from each other and, therefore, necessarily finite. Those concepts cannot, therefore, be used to gain knowledge of that Most Transcendent Reality. He is exalted above the possibility of being known by description, and whoever limits God with a given attribute has failed to gain any knowledge of Him.

By mentioning a few examples we can understand to some degree how the attributes are not superadded to the essence. Take into consideration that the rays of heat proceeding from fire convey heat to everything, so that one of the qualities and attributes of fire is burning and the distribution of heat.

Has this quality occupied one corner of the being of the fire's being? Of course not; the entire being of fire has the attribute of burning and the distribution of heat.

Imam Ja'far as-Sadiq, upon whom be peace, said in answer to someone who was questioning him about the nature of God: "He is something utterly other than all things; He alone is identical with the very essence of being. He is not a body and has no form. The senses cannot perceive Him and He cannot be sought out. He escapes the grasp of the five senses; fantasy and imagination are unable to perceive Him. The passage of time and the succession of ages in no wise diminish Him and He is exempt from all mutation and change."[29]

The Unity of God

When the question of divine unity is raised in religious discourse, it is taken to include many topics including belief in the oneness of the essence, so, too, the compounding of the attributes and the distinction between essence and attributes is totally excluded with respect to unity of the attributes. Distinctness and differentiation derive from limitation. If we posit a difference among the divine attributes, it is valid only from the point of view of our rational thought and reflection; a multiplicity of directions and of superadded attributes cannot affect the divine essence as such.

If in the world of nature we look at a body through different colored pieces of glass, that body will appear to us in a succession of different colors. Similarly, when we contemplate the unique divine essence with our reason, we sometimes ascribe knowledge to that infinite being with regard to the fact that all creatures are at all times present before Him; we then say that He is all-knowing. At other times we are aware of His ability to create all things, and we then speak of His being all-powerful.

So when we perceive through these various apertures, the different attributes which appear to resemble the properties of our limited beings, we attempt to separate them from His infinite essence. Objectively, however, all the concepts conveyed by the different attributes have a single existence and convey a single reality, a reality that is free of all defect and deficiency, that possesses all perfections such as power, mercy, knowledge, blessedness, wisdom and splendor.

Ali, upon whom be peace, the Commander of the Faithful, says in the first sermon of the Nahj *al-balaghah*, "The beginning of religion is the knowledge of the pure divine essence, and the perfection of such knowledge lies in faith in that sacred being. Perfect belief, in turn, lies in sincere devotion at His threshold, and perfect devotion is none other than the dissociation of that Unique Principle from all the attributes of contingent beings.

"Beware, for He cannot be described with any attribute, for then difference would appear between the name and the attribute. Whoever attempts to describe Him with an attribute is, in effect, creating a like and a partner for Him, or rather he is seeing God to be two. Whoever sees God to be two is attempting to divide His being. Such a person lacks all knowledge and insight into the nature of God's unique being and is blind and ignorant.

"The one who is thus deprived of vision will attempt to point to God (i.e., restrict Him to a given time and place), and whoever does this posits imprisoning limits for the Creator of all being and makes Him finite. Whoever limits and restricts Him in this way regards Him as a measurable quantity. Whoever asks: "Where is God?" unintentionally makes of Him a body enclosed within another body, and whoever asks, "In what is God engaged?" unintentionally states that certain places are empty of His being."

So each attribute is infinite and coextensive with the infinitude of the essence. God is free of and exempt from finite attributes that might be distinct from each other and separate from the essence.

Once we realize that God's being derives from Himself, it follows that an absolute being is infinite in all respects. If being and non-being are equally conceivable for an entity, it must acquire being from some external cause to come into being; self-origination is, after all, impossible. It is, then, only absolute being that derives from itself; all other realities are subordinate to it and knowable only by means of it. Once an essence is identical with its own existence, it is infinite with respect to knowledge, power, non-origination and everlastingness, for all of these are forms of being, and an essence that is identical with existence must necessarily possess all these perfections to an infinite degree.

*****

The oneness of God is one of His foremost attributes. All the heavenly religions, in their original and undistorted teachings, have summoned mankind to a pure affirmation of God's unity, untainted by the ascription of partners to Him. Such ascription of partners, in all its forms and dimensions, is the most harmful error to which man is liable. It has occurred throughout history as a result of ignorance, unawareness, and turning away from the guidance of reason and the teaching of the Prophets.

If men believed in God according to correct thought, the proofs of reason and the guidance of the Prophets, it would be impossible for them to accept any contingent phenomenon or created thing in His place, and to imagine that any other being might be His partner or equal in commanding and controlling the destinies of the world, or even have some share in administering the order of the universe.

If numerous gods ruled over the world and each of these gods acted and gave commands in accordance with his own will, the order of the universe would dissolve into anarchy.

The Quran says: *"If there were numerous gods other than the one true God, the order of the heavens and the earth would collapse. So exalted be the Lord of the Throne above what they say concerning Him."* (21:22)

If we say that God is one, it is because He is not a body. A body is a compound of a series of different elements, the union of which causes it to come into being. Compounding, division and generation are all attributes of contingent beings and bodies; we, therefore, negate them in the case of God and assert that whatever has come into existence, as a result of compounding and generation, neither is God nor resembles Him.

It is feasible to conceive of plurality within a given category once we speak of limitations such as quantity, quality, and time. God, however, is not limited by any of these, and it is, therefore, impossible to conceive of Him having any like or congener.

If we try to imagine the essence of water, without any limiting attribute, and repeat this exercise several times, nothing will be added to our original conception. Because in the beginning we conceived of water in an absolute sense, not limited by any condition, quantity or quality, it is impossible that in our subsequent attempts to conceive of it, a new hypothesis should occur to us.

But when we add to the essence of water certain limiting attributes which are extrinsic to it, different forms and instances of water will appear and with them, plurality. Examples of this would be rainwater, springwater, river water, sea water, all of these observed at different times and in different places, here and there. If we eliminate all these limiting attributes and look again at the fundamental essence of water, we will see that it is exempt from all duality and is a single essence.

We must be aware that any being which can be contained in a certain place necessarily has need of that place, and any being that be contained in a certain time owes its very existence to the defining conditions of that time: its existence will be realized only within the specific temporal framework where those conditions obtain.

So, when we come to know a being that is present at all times and in all places and who possesses the highest conceivable degree of perfection, and other than whom nothing is perfect or absolute and free from defect, we must recognize that to impute duality to such a lofty reality is to make it finite and limited.

Indeed, God is not one in a numerical sense so that we might imagine Him to be the first member of a category that is followed by a second. His oneness is such that if we imagine a second to exist with Him, that second must be identical with the first.

Since the multiplicity of things derives from the limiting circumstances that differentiate them from each other, it would be totally irrational to posit a second for a being that is free of all limits and bounds. The existence of a second would mean that the first had limits and bounds, and if limits and bounds are excluded, we cannot possibly have two beings; our conception of the second will simply be a repetition of the first.

The doctrine of divine unity means that if we consider God alone, to the exclusion of all phenomenal being, His sacred essence is completely affirmed. Likewise, if we regard His being together with phenomenal being, again His existence will be completely affirmed. But if, on the contrary, we look at contingent phenomena to the exclusion of God, they cannot in any way be said to be existent, because their existence is dependent on the Creator for its origination and perpetuation.

So, whenever we ascribe some limit and condition to God, it means that God will cease to exist whenever that limit and condition cease to exist. However, God's existence is not subject to condition and plurality, and reason cannot, therefore, posit a second member of His category.

Let us give an illustration. Suppose that the world is infinite— it has no bounds and in whatever direction we travel, we never come to its end. With such a concept of the world of bodies, all of its dimensions being infinite, can we imagine another world to exist in addition to it, whether finite or infinite? Certainly we cannot, because the concept of an infinite world of bodies necessarily excludes the existence of another such world. If we try to conceive of another such world, it will be either identical with the first world or a segment of it.

So, considering that the divine essence is absolute being, to posit the existence of a second being resembling Him is exactly the same as imagining a second world of bodies to co-exist with an infinite world of bodies. In other words, it is impossible.

It is, thus, clear that the meaning of God's being One is not that He is not two; it is that a second is inconceivable and that the exclusive possession of divinity is necessitated by His essence. He becomes distinct from other than Himself, not by means of any limit but by means of His essence itself which can clearly be distinguished from all else. All other beings, by contrast, attain their distinctiveness not from their essence but rather from God.

*****

We see clearly that extensive interrelatedness and harmony exist among all the components of the world. Man produces a carbonic gas that enables plants to breathe, and trees and plants, reciprocally produce oxygen that enables man to breathe. As a result of this interchange between man and plants, a certain amount of oxygen is preserved at all times; were it not to be so, no trace of human life would remain on earth.

The amount of heat received by the earth from the sun corresponds to the need of living beings for heat. The speed of the earth's rotation around the sun and the distance it keeps from that source of energy and heat have been fixed at a level that makes human life on earth possible. The distance of the earth from the sun determines a degree of heat that exactly corresponds to the needs of life upon earth. Were the speed of the earth's rotation to be a hundred miles an hour instead of a thousand miles an hour, as it now is, our nights and days would be ten times as long, and the intensity of the sun's heat would rise to the point that all plant life would be burnt and the cold nights of winter would freeze all fresh shoots in the ground.

If, on the one hand, the rays of the sun were to be reduced by half, all living beings would be frozen in place by the extreme cold. If, on the other hand, they were to be doubled, the sperm of life would never come to fruition. If the moon were farther away from the earth, the tides would become strong and fierce enough to uproot the mountains.

Seen in this light, the world appears to be a caravan in which all the travellers are joined together like links in a chain. All of its parts, big or small, are striving cooperatively to advance in a single direction. Throughout this organism, everything fulfills its particular function and all things aid and complement each other. A profound and invisible link joins every single atom to all other atoms.

A world that is thus replete with unity must necessarily be connected to a single source and principle. Being derives from a single origin; if the entirety of the universe is one, its creator must also be one. The fact that the creator has brought forth unity within the multiplicity of the created world is in itself a convincing proof of His oneness, power and wisdom.

The Quran says: "Ask them, *'Show me these partners whom you worship in place of God. Have they created anything from earth or have they shared with God in the creation of the heavens? Have we given them a book on which they rely in their ascription of partners to us?'* No, the *wrongdoers deceive each other with their false promises. Certainly it is God Who preserves the heavens and the earth from collapse and annihilation; were they about to collapse and be annihilated, there is none other who could preserve them. Know that God is most forbearing and forgiving.*" (35:40-41)

Our innate nature, which is a fundamental dimension of our existence, also confirms the oneness of God. In severe crises and

times of hardship, our desires are all focused on one point; we turn
in one direction and entrust our hearts to Him.

One of the pupils of Imam Ja'far Sadiq, upon whom be peace,
asked him, "What proof is there for the oneness of God?"

The Imam answered him: "The proof of His oneness is the
interrelatedness and continuity of all creation, the integral order of
being that rules over all things. God says in the Quran: *'Were there
a creator in the heavens and earth other than the One God, their order
would vanish and the world would be destroyed.'* "[30]

So the regularity and comprehensiveness of the order that
ruled over all things refutes the theory that there might be several
gods, ruling the same or different spheres.

*****

Although the Quran stresses the unity of God in creation and
wisdom, it also mentions the role of the causes and means that
implement the divine command. It says: *"God sent down water from
the heavens and revived the earth thereby after its death. In that is a clear
sign for men who pay heed."* (16:65)

Once we reach the conclusion that God alone is engaged in
creating, ordering and managing the entire universe, and that all
sources of effect and causality are subordinate to His will and
command, each having its particular role assigned to it by God—
once we reach this conclusion, how can we imagine any other being
to be on the same level as God and bow down in worship before it?
The Quran says: *"Some men regard other beings as equivalent to God
and love them as if they were God but the believers devote all of their love
to God."* (2:165) *"Among His signs are the night and the day and the sun
and the moon. Do not bow down and prostrate yourselves before the sun
and the moon. Instead, prostrate yourselves humbly before the God that
created them."* (41:37)

Lesson Twelve
The Infinite Power of God

The infinite power of God has no clearer proof than that furnished by the study and examination of the phenomena of the created universe and the multiple forms and colorations of nature that can never be fully described.

When we look at God's creation we find ourselves confronted with so vast an energy that no limit can be imagined for it. A look at creation and the millions of truths secreted in the wonders of nature and the depths of man's own being provides the clearest indication of the scale of the power of the One Who has created it, for the rich and complex order of being admits of no other explanation.

It is God's incomparable power that compels man to bow humbly before the Creator of this great scheme. There is no word to express the dimensions of His power; that unique essence has much power that whenever He wills a thing to come into existence, it suffices for the command "*Be!*" to issue forth from Him and the object addressed will be. The Quran says: "*When He wills a certain thing, He commands it 'Be!' and it is.*" (36:82)

The law expounded in this verse is the best indicator of His limitless power and manifestation of His boundless power and splendor. It negates any limit that might be set on God's power and proclaims the inadequacy of all criteria and measures when confronted with this divine law.

The champions of the natural sciences, the men of the laboratory, despite all the advances they have achieved, have not yet gained complete knowledge of the inner secrets of a single one among the numerous and varied beings of the created universe. Nonetheless, the partial and defective knowledge that man has acquired concerning a few of the beings that exist in this world is enough for him to realize with all his being that the great power that has created such variety and abundance in the universe must be infinite.

Consider the range of His creation: tiny creatures and monstrous beasts with strange appearances both dwelling in the depths of the ocean; delicate and melodious birds with multicolored wings, the beauty of which skilled artists imitate as an adornment to their craft; stars that shine in the heavens and the sun that rises and sets; the dawn and the moonlight; the planets, galaxies and nebula each of which sometimes contains at its heart millions of great shinning stars giddying in their apparent infinitude.

Does not a creation such as this, awe inspiring in its splendor, indicate the infinite power of its Maker? Can one disregard the power of a Creator Who imparts such variety to life and made distinct, finite forms of it appear in all this vast range of phenomena?

Now, given the fact that all these captivating forms of creation ultimately arise from the atom, the question of being cannot be explained except by reference to a guiding and infinite power. It is He Who impels all things toward the assumption of life-giving form and possesses the power and intelligence to plan and design this vast and precise scheme.

*****

Large and small, difficult and easy, are properties pertaining to finite beings; in the infinite realm of God's essence and attributes, there is no question of great and little, much and few. Impotence and inability are caused by the finiteness of the energy at the disposal of an agent, by the existence of an obstacle on his path, or by the absence of means and instruments; they are inconceivable in the case of an infinite power.

The Quran says: "*Nothing in the heavens or on earth can induce weakness or impotence in God; indeed, God is all-knowing and all-powerful.*" (35:44)

Although God is capable of doing all things, He has created the world according to a precise and specific scheme in the framework of which a set role has been assigned to certain phenomena in the origination of others. Those phenomena are completely and unquestioningly subordinate to His command while fulfilling that role and never rebelling against His orders in the slightest.

The Quran says: *"The sun, the moon and the stars are all at His command. Be aware that creation belongs only to God; it is His penetrating command that in its exalted purity creates the world and all it contains."* (7:54)

Strictly speaking, no creature in the scheme of the universe can be a manifestation of power or have any share in His will and command, for just as God has no partner in His essence, so, too, He has no partner in His agenthood.

Just as all creatures in the world lack independence in their essence and are dependent on Him, they also lack it in producing acts and effects. Every agent and cause derives the essence of its being from God and also its power to act and produce an effect.

Whenever He wills and necessitates it, the order that encloses all beings abandons its role, for that order is itself subordinate to His will, precious and firm though it may be. The Creator Who has assigned a particular effect to every factor and cause is able to neutralize and suspend that effect at any instant. Just as one command brought the order of the universe into existence, another command robs phenomena of their customary effect.

Thus, the Quran says: *"They said, 'Burn Abraham and thus render help unto your gods, if you are men of action.' We commanded the fire, 'be cool for Abraham and harm him not.' They sought a stratagem against him, but We made them the losers."* (21:68-69)

Although the powerful attraction exerted by the sun and the earth prevails over a vast space, both bodies are subordinate to His will. As soon as He gives a little bird the necessary power, the bird is able to resist the pull of the earth and take flight.

The Quran says: *"Do they not look at the birds in the heavens and see how the skies have been subjugated to them? It is God alone Who keeps them aloft, and in this there is an evident sign of God's power for the people of faith."* (16:79)

Whatever phenomenon may be imagined to exist in the world of being finds its needs for sustenance and life met by the Creator. Therefore, whatever power and capacity is found in the scheme of creation must necessarily go back to the infinite power of God.

Ali, peace be upon him, the Commander of the Faithful, says in a sermon reproduced in the *Nahj al-balaghah*: "O God, we cannot penetrate the depths of Your splendor and majesty. We know only that You are living and self-subsistent, that You are exempt from eating and sleeping. No mind can perceive You and no eye can see You. But You see all eyes, You know the life span of all things, and You are all-powerful.

"Although we have perceived nothing of Your creation, we are astounded by Your power and praise You mightily. That which is hidden from us and our eyes cannot see and our mind and intelligence cannot attain, which is concealed from us by veils of the unseen, is much greater than what we can see..."[31]

When man decides to build something—for example, a hospital—he assembles the necessary tools and pieces of equipment that do not have any essential relationship with each other, and, then, connects them with each other by means of a series of artificial relationships in order to reach his goal.

In order to create such artificial relationships, he makes use of different forces and objects that he finds to be already existing. His work and activity are a part of the system of creation; they are not properly speaking creative activity, but only a form of motion that takes place within existing objects. Divine creation forms a quite different category from the production of artificial relationships between unrelated objects. God originates things with all their properties, forces and energies and characteristics.

When we say that God is all-powerful, we must be aware that His power relates only to things that are possible. Things that are rationally impossible are entirely outside the sphere of His power, and to use the word "power" or "capacity" in connection with things that are impossible is incorrect and meaningless. Although the power of God is, indeed, unlimited, the receptive capacity of things and their ability to serve as locus for the manifestation of divine power must be taken into consideration. The implementation of God's will is intertwined with the relations between cause and effect, with the complex network of reasons and causes. In order for a thing to become the object of the divine will, it must not be impossible and must, in its essence, possess receptive capacity; divine will is accomplished by means of the receptivity of things. It is true that the divine effulgence is infinite and constantly overflowing, but the ground destined to receive it may be defective and unable to absorb the infinite share that superabundant source offers it.

The ocean is an immensely abundant source of water, but a

tanker has only a limited capacity to take on its water; in fact, only a minute amount of that water can be loaded onto a tanker. Clearly enough, what is finite and limited in this case is the capacity of the tanker, not the water in the ocean.

Someone once asked Ali, the Commander of the Faithful, upon whom be peace, "Is your Lord able to fit the whole world into a hen's egg?" He answered: "God Almighty is, indeed, able to do anything, but what you ask is something impossible."[32]

So although God's sacred essence is utterly free of all impotence and inability, it is meaningless and irrational to ask whether God can do something inherently impossible.

*****

One whose heart beats with the love of God and flows over with belief in the Creator of all being will never be discouraged, lonely and hopeless even in the midst of the most complex difficulties. Whatever deed he undertakes he does so in the consciousness of being in the protective shade of a supreme power that can make him triumph over all difficulties.

A man who is aware of God and knows that he enjoys His support can resist and endure all kinds of hardship. Difficulties are for him like foam on swift vanishing foam on the face of the waters. The fire that burns within him becomes ever brighter and he emerges stronger than ever from the crucible of hardship.

Throughout the toils he endures, he is comforted and strengthened by God's kindness and favor, and it is this that forms the true motor of his activity. Failure does not block his path and cause him to surrender; instead, with sincere intention and diligent effort, he continues his strivings until final victory.

He understands well that his efforts cannot remain fruitless and that victory goes to the deserving. Whenever He wills, God takes the hand of the fallen and the oppressed who have no refuge other than Him and raises them up to the apex of power. Sometimes, too, He rubs in the dust of humiliation and disaster the noses of the powerful and arrogant oppressors who believe only in violence and the logic of force and treat men as if they were worthless.

How many arrogant tyrants have been cast down by disaster in the course of human history, sinking and vanishing in a tempest of shame!

The story of God's messengers represents in itself a complete and ideal model of human values. We all know how the messengers stood alone against the oppressive forces of their day in order to guide men to salvation, reform their society, and inculcate lofty values in them. In doing so, they lit the first spark that ultimately destroyed polytheism.

The response aroused by their beliefs caused such a positive tumult that they were able to change the face and direction of history. They laid the foundations of monotheistic worship and established the principles of virtue in the most comprehensive way.

Who can deny the role played by their devotion and faith in the untiring struggle they waged? How far can will power alone take man, and how much can it enable him to endure and sacrifice?

A cursory review of the proud history of the Prophets' lives enables us all to behold, in the most vivid fashion possible, the sincerity and devotion they displayed, their mercy and forbearance, and their intense desire to guide and reform men. The fundamental secret of their success was the fact they never thought of themselves for a single instant; they sincerely renounced their own beings, making them a gift to God's cause. God then responded by bestowing immortality and everlasting fame on them.

Lesson Thirteen
The Boundless Knowledge of God

A Creator Who cannot be circumscribed by place, for Whose Essence no limit is conceivable, of Whose being not a single part of the heavens and earth is empty—such a Creator is naturally aware of all things; there is nothing throughout the whole scheme of being on which the bright rays of His knowledge do not shine.

The events that occur in the most distant part of the universe, happenings that occurred billions of years ago or will occur billions of years in the future—all are contained in the sphere of His knowledge, and the most comprehensive attempts at interpreting His knowledge are, therefore, doomed to failure.

In order to understand the extensive scope of His knowledge, we stretch the limits of our thought, apply our intelligence to reflection and search, and try to advance to our goal with a clear mind. In the last resort, however, our mental apparatus lacks the skills required for reaching the goal.

If we were to exist everywhere in just the same way that we exist at a given place and in a given time, so that no place was deprived of our presence, nothing would be hidden from us and we would be aware of everything.

For us, the world of being has been divided into two sectors: the manifest and the hidden. Things are "hidden" in the sense that certain truths, being infinite and non-material, cannot be perceived by the outer senses. It is important to remember that the entirety of existence does not consist of matters that lie within the range of the empirical sciences.

In order to understand the secrets and mysteries of creation we need, as it were, a launch platform. The elevation we are able to reach depends on the intellectual force we have at our disposal and the degree of understanding that propels our ascent. Once we have a suitable launch platform, many realities become knowable to us.

*****

Through its use of the term *ghayb* ("hidden"), the Noble Quran sets before man a broad vision of reality. God's messengers have also striven to raise man's awareness of the created universe to a level that embraces infinite as well as the finite and the boundaries of the unseen as well as the dimensions of the manifest.

For God, the "hidden" does not exist; for Him, the universe is entirely "manifest." The Quran says: *"He is the Knower of the Hidden and the Manifest, the Compassionate and the Merciful."* (59:22)

Whatever is made by man derives from the skill, intelligence and knowledge of its maker. The more subtle and refined the product, the more clearly it displays the profound and extensive knowledge of its maker, and the more fully it proves his ability to plan and design.

Man's handiwork is not in any way comparable to the mysteries and splendor of creation. Nonetheless, it suggests to us that the harmonious and orderly scheme of the universe, and the manifestatior of intelligence in this vast, beautiful and astounding pattern of creation, must necessarily indicate that the one who plans it and endows it with order must possess boundless and comprehensive knowledge. The orderliness of the universe is the strongest proof for the existence of a being that overflows with the knowledge, will, awareness and wisdom and has designed the wonders of creation in accordance with a precisely calculated plan. The signs of His infinite knowledge are to be seen plainly in every particle of every phenomenon.

The experiments and theories of scientists furnish proof for who ever desires it of the boundless knowledge of God and its countless manifestations in the insect, animal and vegetable realms.

God is aware of the course of the stars in space, the tumult-ridden world of the nebulae and the rotation of the galaxies; of all things from pre-eternity to post-eternity; of the total number of atoms in all the heavenly bodies; of the motions of the billions of creatures, large and small, that move on the face of the earth and in the depths of the oceans; of the norms and laws that unfailingly regulate nature; of the hidden and manifest aspects of all things. He even knows the perplexities of the distraught better than they do themselves.

Listen again to what the Quran has to say: *"Is not the one who created the world aware of the secrets of His own creation? Certainly He has knowledge of all the subtleties and mysteries of the world."* (67:14) *"Nothing is hidden from God, neither on earth nor in the heavens."* (3:5)

Natural scientists are better acquainted than others with the subtle and precise mysteries that are implanted in every particle of creation; they are aware from their studies and researches of the various calculations that are built into things both living and lifeless, in cells and globules; of the various forms of action and reaction, outward and inward, that take place in them; and of the effects of various materials and substances. Thus, they witness the signs fo God's astounding wisdom and infinite knowledge in nature or, as the Quran puts it, *"...on the horizons."* (41:53) More than others, they are exposed to the manifestation of God's attributes and perfections, including His unbounded knowledge, and if they do not reject the call of their conscience, they will also discern the existence of the Creator more clearly.

A certain thinker once said, "Our world resembles a great idea more than it does a great machine. As a theory or a scientific definition, it can be said that the world is the product of a great idea, the manifestation of a thought and an idea superior to our own. Scientific thought seems to be moving in the direction of this theory."

God's knowledge is not restricted to things past or to present events and objects; His knowledge of the future is exactly like His knowledge of the present.

God's knowledge is, so to speak, "immediate" in the complete sense of the word. It is not in the first instance necessary that there should be an object of knowledge to Which His knowledge should attach itself. All things stand revealed before Him, for at the very same time that His sacred essence is utterly other than all creatures and phenomena, it is also not separate from them: all things past and future are in His unmediated presence.

Ali, upon whom be peace, the Commander of the Faithful, says: "He knows all things, but not through means and instruments, the absence of which would entail the cessation of His knowledge. There is not some added entity called 'knowledge' interposed between Him and the objects of His knowledge; there is nothing but

His essence alone."[33]

Here, Ali, peace be upon him, is referring to the theological principle that God's awareness of things is direct and immediate. In His knowledge of phenomena, God has no need of the mental forms that are the basis of acquired knowledge. Were He to acquire His knowledge by means of those forms, need would arise in Him, whereas He is utterly free of need.

The one from whom the existence of the world and its inhabitants derives, who is capable of meeting every imaginable need, who grants every perfection and bounty—is it all conceivable that He should Himself be imprisoned by Need?

Mental forms remain in our minds only so long as we wish them to exist; they disappear as soon as we withdraw our attention from them, because they are fashioned and created by us. This form of knowledge is not direct and unmediated and it is, therefore, termed "acquired knowledge," by contrast with "immediate knowledge," that has no need of a means.

The difference between us, who create our own mental forms and the Creator Who originated all being, lies in this, that we owe our very existences to Him and, therefore, stand in need of Him, whereas He is the true Creator and vivifier of all things, is free of need, and does not need the exercise of vision to acquire knowledge.

The delineation of past and future events that takes place on the horizons of our being and thought is inevitably limited, since we occupy a given time and space outside of which we have no existence. We are material phenomena, and matter, according to the laws of physics and relativity, needs time and place in its gradual and continuous process of development and change. Past and future have no meaning for a being who is present from pre-eternity to post-eternity, in all places and at all times and free from the captivity of matter and its consequences.

Since every phenomenon relies on the infinite existence of the Creator for its origin and existence, no veil or barrier can be supposed to exist between God and that phenomenon; God encompasses its inner and outer dimensions and is utterly empowered over it.

Someone once asked Ali, upon whom be peace, the Commander of the Faithful, "Where is God?"

Ali answered: "It is not correct to ask where God is because it is God Who made place. Nor is it correct to ask how God is, of what nature is God, since it is God Who created all nature. Further, it is not correct to ask what God is because it is God Who created all quiddity.

"Glorified be God Almighty in the waves of Whose splendor the wise are unable to swim, the remembrance of Whose eternity halts all thought in its track, and in Whose vast heaven of sanctity the intellect loses its way!"[34]

The Quran says: ' *God is aware of all that exists on the face of the earth and in the depths of the oceans. He knows of every leaf that falls and every seed that is hidden in the darkness of the earth. All things, fresh and dry, are clear and evident to Him.*" (6:59)

Let us imagine that we are in a room overlooking the street and watching through a small window the mass of cars that swiftly moves down the street. Obviously we cannot see all the cars at once; we see them one by one as they pass in front of the window, and then they disappear from sight. If we knew nothing about cars, we might imagine that they gradually come into being on one side of the window and cease to exist on the other.

Now this small window corresponds exactly to our field of vision; it determines a past and a future for the cars. Those who are outside the room standing on the sidewalk see all the cars moving along together.

Our situation with respect to the past and future of the world is like that of the person watching the cars through a small window.

Once we realize that God is above time and place, we understand that all past and future events are always present and existent in front of Him, like a painting.

We ought, therefore, to have a sense of responsibility toward a Creator Who is aware of the slightest act and deed of creation—as the Quran says: "He *knows all that you do*" (2:283)—and avoid any sin or mistake that would cause us to become distant from Him. We ought to worship God, the possessor of absolute knowledge Who has caused us to traverse these various stages and to attain the capacities we now have. We ought not to disobey His commands Which open up for us the path to true felicity and the ultimate aim of man, and we should accept no goal other than Him.

In order to reach God we must adorn ourselves with divine attributes and prepare ourselves, during our brief sojourn in this world, for the meeting with Him. Then we may return to Him, the source, origin and beginning of our existence. This requires action and striving effort aimed at refining the self, for the responsibility to act in this sense has been placed on man's shoulders as a divine trust.

Lesson Fourteen
Opinions Concerning God's Justice

The problem of justice as one of God's attributes has had its own distinct history. Various schools of thought in Islam have held different views on the subject, interpreting it in accordance with their own distinctive principles.

Some Sunnis who follow the views of the theologian Abu'l-Hasan Ash'ari do not believe in God's justice as a matter of faith, and they deny that justice is accomplished by the divine acts.

In their view, however, God treats a certain person, and whatever punishment or reward He gives him, irrespective of what he might appear to deserve, will represent justice and absolute good, even though it might appear unjust when measured by human standards.

These Ash'aris, thus, distinguish God's attribute of justice from His acts and they, therefore, regard as just whatever can be attributed to God. If He rewards the virtuous and punishes the sinful, this is justice, but so would be the reverse; it would still be in the broad sphere of His justice.

Their claim that the very terms "justice" and "injustice" are meaningless when applied to God is no doubt intended to elevate God's most sacred essence to the position of the highest transcendence. But no thoughtful person will regard these superficial and inadequate notions as having anything to do with God's transcendence. In fact, they involve a denial of order in the world, of the principle of causality both in the general order of the world and in the conduct and deeds of individual men.

The followers of al-Ash'ari believe, moreover, that the bright lamp of the intellect is extinguished whenever it is confronted with the perceptions and problems of religion, that it is unable to benefit man or light up his path.

This claim conforms neither to the teachings of the Quran nor to the content of the sunnah. The Quran considers disregard for the intellect to be a form of misguidance and repeatedly summons men to reflection and meditation in order to learn divine knowledge and religious beliefs. Those who fail to benefit from this bright lamp within them are compared to the animals. The Quran says: *"The worst of creatures in the sight of God are those persons who are deaf and dumb and do not reflect."* (8:22)

The Prophet of Islam says: "God has assigned two guides to man: one external to him, the messengers of God, and the other internal, his own power of thought.

*****

The Mutazilites and Shi'a stand in opposition to al-Ash'ari and his school. Out of all the attributes of God, they have selected justice to be a principle of their creed. Relying on both transmitted and rational proofs, they have also refuted and rejected as incompatible with the principle of justice, the doctrines of the unmediated effect of divine destiny and the predetermination of man's acts.

They believe that justice is the basis of God's acts, both in the ordering of the universe and in the establishing of laws. Just as human acts can be weighed according to the criteria of good and bad, the acts of the Creator are also subject to the same criteria. Since the logic of reason determines that justice is inherently praiseworthy and injustice inherently reprehensible, an object of worship whose characteristics include infinite intelligence and spirit, will never undertake an act that reason regards as impermissible.

When we say that God is just, it means that His all-knowing and creative essence does nothing that is contrary to wisdom and benefit. The concept of wisdom, when applied to the Creator, does not mean that He chooses the best means for attaining His goals or remedying His deficiencies, for it is only man who is called on to move from deficiency toward perfection. God's concern is to make beings emerge from deficiency and impel them toward perfection and the aims inherent in their own essences. God's wisdom consists of this, that He first implants a form of His favor within each phenomenon, and then, after bestowing existence upon it, impels it toward the perfection of its capacities through a further exercise of His generosity.

Justice has, then, an extensive meaning, which naturally includes the avoidance of oppression and all foolish acts. Imam Ja'far as-Sadiq, peace be upon him, says in explanation of God's justice: "Justice in the case of God means that you should not ascribe anything to God that if you were to do it would cause you to be blamed and reproached."[35]

With man, oppression and all the forms of corrupt activity in which he engages, derive, without doubt, from ignorance and lack of awareness and need coupled with innate lowliness; sometimes, too, they are the reflection of hatred and enmity, which leap forth from man's inner being like a spark.

Numerous are those people who are disgusted with their own oppressiveness and corruption. Nonetheless, because of ignorance about the final outcome of their deeds, they continue, from time to time, to act with injustice and pollute themselves with all kinds of shameful, corrupt deeds.

Sometimes man feels that he needs something that he does not have the resources or ability to acquire. This is the root cause of many evils. The feeling of need, hunger and greed, the prevalence in man of a desire to harm or dominate—all these are factors leading to aggressive behavior.

Under their influence, man loses the reins of self-control. He concentrates all his efforts on fulfilling his desires and violating all ethical restrictions, he starts squeezing the throats of the oppressed.

The unique essence of God, that infinite being, is free of all such tendencies and limitations, for nothing is hidden from His knowledge without bound, and it is inconceivable that He should suffer from impotence vis-a-vis anything—He, the Pre-Eternal One Whose eternal rays bestow life and sustenance on all things and Who assures their movement, variety and development.

A subtle essence that comprehends all the degrees of perfection stands in no need of anything so that its absence might induce anxiety in Him when He conceives a desire for it. His power and capacity are without any doubt, unlimited and they do not fall short of anything so that He might then be led to deviate from the path of justice and transgress against someone, or take vengeance in order to quieten his heart or undertake some inappropriate and ill-sided act.

None of the motivations for unjust behavior can be found in

God, and, indeed, the very concepts of oppression and injustice are inapplicable to a being Whose generosity and mercy embrace all things and the sanctity of Whose essence is clearly manifest throughout creation.

The Quran repeatedly negates all idea of injustice by God, considering Him in His sanctity utterly removed from all unworthy acts. It says: *"God never considers it permissible to act unjustly toward His servants; it is rather men who commit oppression and injustice."* (10:44)

In this verse, God dissociates Himself from all notion of injustice, something repugnant to men, and, instead, attributes it to them.

In addition, how is it possible that God should call on men to establish justice and equity while at the same time staining His own hands with unrighteous deeds? The Quran says: *"God commands men to act with justice and virtue and enjoins upon them generosity to kinsfolk. He forbids them evil deeds and oppression. He admonishes you out of His mercy, so that you may accept His advice."* (16:90)

Islam values justice so highly that if one group of Muslims wish to deviate from the path of justice and start engaging in oppression, they must be repressed, even if this involves war. This is the command of the Quran: *"If two parties of believers fight with each other, make peace between them. If one of them has committed aggression against the other, then make war on the aggressor until he returns to observance of God's command. Once he has so returned, then reconcile them and make peace in utter justice. Certainly God loves the just."* (49:9)

The interesting point that emerges from this verse is that the mediator is strictly instructed to make sure, when bringing about reconciliation, that the dispute is settled in accordance with justice, without showing lenience to the aggressor. It may happen, in cases where war has been started for aggressive purposes, that a mediator tries to end the dispute by insisting on leniency and the overlooking of faults, and, ultimately, persuades one of the parties to renounce its claim in favor of the other. This lenient approach, although legitimate in itself, may reinforce the spirit of aggressiveness existing in those who gained by starting the war. It is, in fact, conventional to satisfy the aggressor in such cases by granting him some concession.

Although the voluntary renunciation of one's claim is a desirable act in itself, it will, under such circumstances, have an undesirable effect on the mentality of the aggressor. The aim of Islam is to uproot force and injustice from Islamic society and to assure its members that no one can gain anything by aggression and force.

*****

If we look at the order of creation, we can see that a vast and comprehensive equilibrium prevails among all physical phenomena. This is evident in the regularity of the atoms, the haste of the electrons, the rotation of the planets, and the movements of all bodies. It is visible in the mineral and vegetable realms, in the precise relations that exist among the organs of a living being, in the balance among the inner components of the atom, in the equilibrium among the vast heavenly bodies and their finely calculated forces of attraction. All these forms of balance and equilibrium, together with the other precise laws that science is still seeking to explore, bear witness to the existence of an undeniable order in the universe, one which is confirmed by mathematical equations.

Our veracious Prophet has expressed this universal justice and comprehensive equilibrium—the fact that nothing is irregular or out of place—in this concise and eloquent statement: "It is true equilibrium and symmetry that maintain the earth and the heavens."

The Quran attributes the following words to Moses, peace be upon him and our Prophet: "*Our God is the one who endowed all things with the needful and then guided them for the continuation of their existence.*" (20:50)

In this short sentence, Moses expounds to the Pharaoh the manner in which the world was created together with its orderliness and beauty, which are among God's signs. His aim was to save him from his erroneous thoughts and help him perceive the existence of a just and divinely instituted order in the universe.

One of the norms ruling ineluctably over nature is, therefore, order and justice, and all things, by virtue of their subordination to the norms and laws of nature, are engaged in the process of evolution toward perfection that is specific to each of them. Any deviation from this universal pattern of order and the relations founded upon it would result in confusion and chaos.

Whenever some irregularity occurs in nature, phenomena themselves evince a reaction, and inward or outward factors emerge to remove the barriers to development and re-establish the order needed to continue on the path to perfection.

When the body is attacked by microbes and other factors of illness, white globules begin to neutralize them, in accordance with ineluctable norm. Whatever medicine may be prescribed is an external factor aiding the white globules in their task of neutralization and re-establishing equilibrium in the body.

Finally, it is impossible that God, Whose love is infinite and Who unstintingly grants His favors to His servants, should perform the slightest unjust or inappropriate act. This is, indeed, what the Quran proclaims: *"It is God Who has made the earth a place of abode for you, Who has raised the heavens, created you in the best of forms, and given you delicious and pleasing foods as sustenance. This is God, your Lord."* (40:64)

Lesson Fifteen
An Analysis of Misfortune and Hardship

The question of God's justice involves certain problems, such as the existence of disasters, loss and evil in the natural order, and inequalities in the social order. This question arouses, in fact, a whole storm of questions and objections in the minds of many people. The problems they face are so fundamental that what start out as doubts and hesitations, ultimately become an indissoluble complex.

Such people ask how it is possible that in a world created on the basis of intelligence and wisdom, so much suffering, pain and evil should prevail; that the world should be subjected constantly to the successive blows of hardship and misfortune, with loss and deficiency always in the ascendant.

Why is it that in various parts of the world, terrible, overwhelming events assault mankind, resulting in untold loss and destruction? Why is one person ugly and another beautiful, one healthy and another sick? Why are all men not created equal, and does not their inequality point to an absence of justice in the universe?

Justice in the order of things depends on its being free of oppression, discrimination and disaster, or the absence from it of all defect, sickness, and poverty; this, they say, alone would result in perfection and justice.

*****

We must begin by admitting that our evaluation of the affairs of the universe does not permit us to penetrate the ultimate depths of phenomena; it is inadequate for the analysis of the ends and purposes of things.

Our initial understanding of unpleasant events and disasters is bound to be superficial; we are not prepared to recognize any truth lying beyond our initial impression. We cannot, at the outset, delineate the ultimate aims of those events, and we, therefore, regard them as signs of injustice. Our feelings become aroused and lead us into the most illogical analyses.

But if we reflect more profoundly, we will see that this one-sided evaluation of events we label injustice comes from making our interests or those of people to whom we are directly or indirectly related, our criterion and yardstick. Whatever secures our interests is good, and whatever harms us is bad. In other words, our judgment of good and bad is based on a short-eyed perception, narrow horizons of thought, and a lack of precise knowledge concerning the norms of creation.

Is our existence the only issue involved in every occurrence? Can we make our own profit and loss into the criterion of good and evil? Our material world is constantly engaged in producing change. Events that did not exist today will occur tomorrow; some things will disappear and others will take their place.

It is obvious that what is useful and beneficial for some people today will cease to exist tomorrow. But for us who are human beings and attached to our own existence and the things of the world, the acquisition of things is good and their loss is bad. But despite man and his attachments, the changing nature of the world produces constantly changing phenomena. If the world did not comprehend the possibility of change, phenomena themselves would not exist, and, therefore, there could also be no question of good and evil.

In such a hypothetical, unchanging world there would be neither loss and deficiency nor growth and development, no contrast or differentiation, no variety or multiplicity, no compounding or motion. In a world without deficiency or loss, there would also be no human, moral or social criteria, limits, or laws. Development and change are the result of the motion and rotation of the planets; if they ceased to exist, there would be no earth, no moon and no sun, no day, no month and no year.

*****

A somewhat comprehensive view of the world will permit us to understand that what is harmful for us today, or may be so in the future, is beneficial for others. The world as a whole moves in the direction dictated by the overall purpose of being and benefit of being; individuals may suffer harm in this process, and it may even be that mankind at large does not stand to benefit.

Were we able to plunge deeply enough into the ocean of knowledge and turn the pages of its book replete with mysteries with the finger of our understanding, the ultimate purpose and outcome of all events and phenomena would be revealed to us. However, our power of judgment is not sufficiently comprehensive to deal with the complex web that confronts us: we know neither the chain of preceding causes that have produced the phenomena of today, nor the chain of future effects those phenomena, in turn, will produce.

If it were possible for us to look down from above on the broad plain of the world, in such a way that we could see all the positive and negative aspects of everything, all the mysteries of everything occurring in the world; if it were possible for us to evaluate the effects and results of every event in history, past, present and future and everything occurring between pre-eternity and post-eternity, and, if this were possible for us, then we might be able to say that the harm of a given event outweighed its benefit and brand it as evil.

But does man have such comprehensive awareness of the horizontal and vertical chains of causality? Can he situate himself on the moving axis of the world?

Since we do not dispose of such an ability, since we will never be able to traverse so infinite a distance, however long be our stride; since we will never be able to lift the veil from all these complexities and take their due measure, it is best that we refrain from one-sided and hasty judgments that are based on our own short-sightedness. We should recognize that we must not make our own benefit the sole criterion for judging this vast universe. The relative observations we make within the framework of the limited data at our disposal and the specific conditions to which we are subject can never furnish criteria for a definitive judgment.

Nature may often be working toward the fulfillment of a particular goal that is unimaginable to man, given his conventional circumstances. Why cannot it not be supposed that unpleasant occurrences are the result of efforts aimed at preparing the ground for a new phenomenon that will be the instrument of God's will upon earth? It may be that the conditions and circumstances of the age necessitate such processes.

If all the changes and upheavals that terrify us did not take place within a given plan and design and for the sake of a specific aim, if they were to be extended throughout time without producing any positive or constructive result, there would be no trace on earth of any living creature, including man.

Why should we accuse the world of injustice, of being chaotic and unstable, simply because of a few exceptional occurrences and phenomena in nature? Should we start objecting because of a handful of unpleasantnessess, major and minor, forgetting all the manifestations of precision and wisdom, all the wonders we see in the world and its creatures, that testify to the will and intelligence of an exalted being?

Since man sees so much evidence of careful planning throughout the universe, he must admit that the world is a purposive whole, a process moving toward perfection. Every phenomenon in it is subject to its own specific criterion, and if a phenomenon appears inexplicable or unjustifiable, this is because of man's short-sightedness. Man must understand that in his finiteness, he lacks the capacity to understand the aims of all phenomena and their content; it is not that creation has any defect.

Our attitude to the bitter and unpleasant occurrences of this world resemble the judgment made by a desert dweller when he comes to the city and sees powerful bulldozers destroying old buildings. He regards this demolition as a foolish act of destruction, but is it logical on his part to think that the demolition is unplanned and purposeless? Of course not, because he sees only the process of demolition, not the calculations and plans of the architects and others involved.

As a certain scientist said: "Our state is like that of children who watch a circus packing up and preparing to move on. This is necessary for the circus to go elsewhere and continue with its life of excitement, but those short-sighted children see in the folding of the tents and the comings and goings of men and animals nothing but the dissolution and termination of the circus."

*****

If we look a little more deeply and imaginatively at the misfortunes and disasters that plague man and interpret them correctly, we will appreciate that in reality, they are blessings, not disasters. A blessing being a blessing, and a disaster being a disaster is dependent upon man's reaction to it; a single event may be experienced quite differently by two different people.

Misfortune and pain are like an alarm warning man to remedy his deficiencies and errors; they are like a natural immune system or regulatory mechanism inherent in man.

If wealth leads to self-indulgence and pleasure-seeking, it is a misfortune and a disaster, and if poverty and deprivation lead to the refinement and development of the human soul, they are a blessing. Thus, wealth cannot be counted as absolute good fortune nor poverty as absolute misfortune. A similar rule covers whatever natural gifts man may possess.

Nations who are confronted by various hostile forces and compelled to struggle for their survival are strengthened thereby. Once we regard effort and struggle to be a positive and constructive endeavor, we cannot overlook the role played by hardships in developing man's inner resources and impelling him to progress.

People who are not obliged to struggle and who live in an environment free of all contradiction will easily be immersed by material prosperity in their pleasures and lusts.

How often it happens that someone willingly endures hardship and pain for the sake of a great goal! Were it not for that hardship and pain, the goal might not appear so desirable to him! A smooth path along which one advances blindly and mechanically is not conducive to development and growth, and a human effort from which the element of conscious will has been removed cannot produce a fundamental change in man.

Struggle and contradiction are like a scourge impelling man forward. Solid objects are shattered by the pressure of repeated blows, but men are formed and tempered by the hardships they endure. They throw themselves into the ocean to learn how to swim, and it is in the furnace of crisis that genius emerges.

Untrammeled self-indulgence, love of the world, unrestricted pleasure-seeking, heedlessness of higher goals—all these are indications of misguidance and lack of awareness. In fact, the most wretched of men are those who have grown up in the midst of luxury and comfort, who have never experienced the hardships of life or tasted its bitter days along with the sweet: the sun of their lives rises and sets within, unnoticed by anyone else.

Following one's inclinations and adhering to one's desires is incompatible with firmness and elevation of spirit, with purposeful effort and striving. Pleasure-seeking and corruption, on the one hand, and strength of will and purposiveness, on the other, represent two contrary inclinations in man. Since neither can be negated or affirmed to the exclusion of the other, one must strive constantly to reduce the desire for pleasure and strengthen the opposing force within one.

Those who have been raised in luxury, who have never tasted the bitter and sweet days of the world, who have always enjoyed prosperity and never endured hunger—they can never appreciate the taste of delicious food nor the joy of life as a whole and they are incapable of truly appreciating beauty. The pleasures of life can be truly enjoyed only by those who have experienced hardship and failure in their lives, who have the capacity to absorb difficulty and to endure those hardships that lie in wait along every step of man's path.

Material and spiritual ease become precious to man only after experiencing the ups and downs of life and the pressure of its unpleasant incidents.

Once man is preoccupied with his material life, all dimensions of his existence are enchained, and he loses aspiration and motion. Inevitably, he will also neglect his eternal life and inward purification. As long as desire casts its shadow on his being and his soul is ensnared by darkness, he will be like a speck tossed around on the waves of matter. He will seek refuge in anything but God. He therefore needs something to awaken him and induce maturity in his thoughts, to remind him of the transitoriness of this ephemeral world and help him attain the ultimate aim of all heavenly teachings—the freedom fo the soul from all the obstacles and carriers that prevent man from attaining lofty perfection.

The training and refinement of the self is not to be had cheaply; it requires the renunciation of various pleasures and enjoyments, and the process of cutting loose from them is bitter and difficult.

It is true that such exertions will be for the sake of purifying man's inner being and allowing his latent capacities to appear. Nonetheless, patient abstention from sin and pleasure-seeking is always bitter to man's taste and it is only through obstinate resistance to lower impulses that he can fulfill his mission of breaking down the barriers that confront him and thus ascend to the realm of higher values.

Lesson Sixteen
Hardship, a Cause of Awakening

Those who are drunk on the arrogance of power and success and who have totally forgotten humane ethics because of the seduction of their soul and their senses will sometimes find, in various corners of the world, that the occurrence of unpleasant events makes them open to fundamental changes and developments that tear away from them the veils of forgetfulness. They may even be guided to a path leading to some degree of moral perfection and a future more fruitful than their present. They are people in whom misfortune has induced a profound transformation.

Considering the harmful effects of neglectfulness and the intoxication of arrogance, on the one hand, and the numerous moral lessons taught by misfortune, on the other, it can be said that failure and misfortune are relative insofar as they contain great blessings; they contribute fruitfully to the building of man's awareness and will.

Hardship is, then, the preliminary to higher, more advanced states of being; it prepares man for the recompense that awaits him, and from his response to it, it becomes apparent whether he has attained the lofty degree of sincerity and devotion or is sunk in decay. The Quran says: *"We have created man in the embrace of hardship."* (90:4) Or, again: *"We test you with fear, hunger, the loss of wealth and possessions, death, and the loss of the fruits of your toil . Give glad tidings to those who struggle manfully on this path that those who say when afflicted with calamity and pain, 'We are from God and to Him we return on our path to perfection,'—that it is they who receive kindness and mercy from their Lord together with their suffering, and they it is who are truly guided."* (2:155-57)

Without doubt, God could have created a world without hardship, pain and misfortune, but that would have meant His depriving man of freedom and choice; he would have been let loose in the world as a creature without will or the power of decision, just like any other creature lacking perception and awareness, formed exclusively by nature and totally obedient to it. Would he then have deserved the name of man?

Having paid the heavy price of losing all his innate capacities and freedom, his most precious resource, would he have advanced toward perfection, or decayed and declined? Would not the world, too, have lost all goodness and beauty, these being comprehensible only in terms of their opposites?

It is plain that the power to distinguish and discriminate makes possible the existence of good and evil, of beauty and ugliness. By giving man the inestimable blessing of freedom and the ability to choose, God, whose wisdom is manifest throughout creation, wished to display fully His ability to create phenomena bearing witness to His wisdom and power.

He placed within man's being the possibility of doing both good and evil, and although He compels him to do neither, He always expects him to do good. God does not approve of evil; it is righteous conduct that meets with His approval and, in exchange for which He provides abundant, unimaginable reward. God warns man against following the path of evil and threatens him with punishment and torment if he does so.

Thus, by using the power of choice that God has bestowed on him, man can act as he should, conforming both to divine guidance and to his own conscience.

But, if occasionally his foot should slip and he should commit some sin, the path remains open for him to return to purity and light, to God's favor and mercy. This is in itself a further manifestation of God's generosity and all-embracing justice, one more of the blessings He bestows on His servants.

Were God to give immediate reward to the virtuous for their righteous conduct and acts, they would not in any way be superior to the corrupt and the sinful. And if the evil in thought and in deed were to be always met with instant punishment and retribution, virtue and purity would not enjoy any superiority in this world to vice and impurity.

*****

The principle of contradiction, is, in fact, the basis of the created world; it is what enables matter to change and evolve so that God's grace flows through the world. Were matter not to take on different shapes as a result of its encounter with various beings and were being unable to accommodate new forms within itself, the differentiation and advancement of being would be impossible. A stable and unchanging world would resemble stagnant capital that produces no profit. For creation, change is the capital that brings about profit. It is, of course, possible that the investment of a certain portion of capital should result in loss, but the constant motion of matter as a whole definitely results in profit. The contradiction that takes place in the forms of matter results in the advancement of the order of being toward perfection.

There is some question as to whether evil exists in the world in the real sense of the word. If we look carefully, we will see that the evil of things is not a true attribute; it is a relative one.

Firearms in the hands of my enemy are an evil for me, and firearms in my hands are an evil for my enemy. Setting aside me and my enemy, firearms are in themselves neither good nor bad.

The course of nature can be said to be mathematical; that is, its system has been established in such a way as not to answer all of our needs. We, however, wish to fulfill all our uncountless desires without encountering the least hindrance, and the forces of nature do not answer the limitless wishes we cherish, wishes which are in any event worthless from the point of view of our essential nature. Nature pays no attention to our desires and refuses to submit to our wants. So when we encounter unpleasantness in our lives, we become unjustifiably upset and we term the causes of our discomfort as "evil."

If someone wants to light his lamp when there is no oil in it, he will not start sighing and complaining or curse the whole universe!

Creation is constantly advancing toward a clear goal, through unceasing effort and striving. Specific causes determine each step it takes, and the changes and development it undergoes are not designed to meet men's approval or satisfy their desires.

It should be accepted that some of the occurrences of this world will not correspond to our wishes, and we ought not to regard as injustice things we experience as unpleasant.

Ali, peace be upon him, the Commander of the Faithful, describes the world as an abode of hardship, but nonetheless a good place for the one who knows it properly. Although he encountered himself all kinds of hardship and unpleasantness, he constantly drew men's attention to the absolute justice of God.35a

Another important point which must not be overlooked is that good and evil do not represent two mutually exclusive categories or series in the order of creation. Goodness is identical with being, and evil is identical with non-being; wherever being makes its appearance, non-existence is also implied.

When we speak of poverty, indigence, ignorance or disease we should not imagine that they have separate realities: poverty is simply not having wealth, ignorance is the absence of knowledge, and disease is the loss of health. Wealth and knowledge are realities, but poverty is nothing other than the emptiness of the hand and the pocket, and ignorance, the absence of knowledge. Hence poverty and ignorance have no tangible reality; they are defined through the non-existence of other things.

The same is the case with calamities and misfortunes that we regard as evil and the source of suffering. They, too, are a kind of loss or non-being, and are evil only in the sense that they result in the destruction or non-existence of something other than themselves. Apart from this, nothing, insofar as it exists, can in any way be called evil or ugly.

If calamities did not entail sickness and death, the loss and ruin of certain creatures, thus preventing their capacities from unfolding, they would not be bad. It is the loss and ruin arising from misfortunes that is inherently bad. Whatever exists in the world is good; evil pertains to non-being, and since non-being does not form a category independent of being, it has not been created and does not exist.

Being and non-being are like the sun and its shadow. When a body is turned to the sun, it casts a shadow. What is a shadow? The shadow has not been created by anything; it consists simply of the sun not shining in a given place because of the existence of an obstacle; it has no source or origin of its own.

Things have a real existence by virtue of having been created without reference to things other than them; in this sense, they are not evil. For a worldview derived from belief in God, the world is equivalent to good. Everything is inherently good; if it is evil, it is so only in a relative sense and in connection with things other than itself. The existence of everything is unreal for other than itself, and untouched by creation.

The malarial mosquito is not evil in itself. If it is described as such, it is because it is harmful to man and causes disease. That which is created is the existence of a thing in and of itself, which is a true existence; speculative or conditional existence has no place in the order of being and is not real. We cannot, therefore, ask why God has created relative or conditional existence. Conditional or abstract entities are inseparable from the real entities that give rise to them; they are their inevitable concomitants and do not partake of their being. One cannot then speak of conditional entities having been created.

That which is real must necessarily derive its being from the Creator. Only those things and attributes are real that exist outside the mind. Relative attributes are created by the mind and have no existence outside it so one cannot go looking for the creator.

Furthermore, that which has the potential to exist is the world as a whole, with all the objects it contains and the attributes that are inseparable from it; the world represents an indivisible unit. From the vantage point of God's wisdom, either the world must exist on the pattern that is peculiar to it, or it cannot exist at all.

A world without order or lacking the principle of causality, a world where good and evil were not separate from each other, would be an impossibility and a fantasy. It is not possible to suppose that one part of the world should exist and another should not. Creation is a whole, like the form and figure of man, and its parts are inseparable from each other.

God is absolutely free of all need, and one consequence of this is that He freely bestows being, like a generous man whose largess expects no return, or like a skilled artist who is constantly busy with the creation of new forms. Such abundant generosity and creativity define the essence of the Lord Whose signs are manifest and evident in every phenomenon.

Lesson Seventeen
Some Aspects of Inequality

Suppose that the owner of a factory employs both skilled and un-skilled workers to operate and administer his factory. When it is time to pay their wages, he pays the skilled and qualified workers, whose job is at a higher level, more than the unskilled workers. Now, is this difference in wages just or unjust? Is the factory owner acting equitably or inequitably?

Doubtless there is a difference involved here, but we cannot call it discrimination. Justice does not require the factory owner to pay unskilled workers the same as skilled workers. It means rather that he should give to each category what it deserves. Such a rule will clearly delineate the comparative value of each job and contribute to the welfare of the workplace.

To make distinctions in such cases is an eloquent and practical form of justice; not to do so would be equivalent to oppression, discrimination and injustice; it would be the result of an inadequate appreciation of the relative value of things in their differentiation.

When we look at the world as a whole and analyze its various parts, we see that each part has its own special position and function and is clothed in the qualities that are suitable to it. In the light of this realization, we can understand the necessity of vicissitudes in human life, of light and darkness, of success and failure, for maintaining the general equilibrium of the world.

If the world were to be uniform, without variation or differ-ence, the varied and multiple species of being would not exist. It is precisely in this abundant variety and multiplicity that do exist that we see the splendor and magnificence of the world. Our judgment of things will be logical, correct, and acceptable when we take into consideration the equilibrium prevailing in the universe and the interrelations that beneficially bind its various parts to each other, not when we examine the part in isolation form the whole.

The order of creation is based on equilibrium, on receptivities and capacities; what is firmly established in creation is differentiation, not discrimination. This observation makes it possible for us to examine the matter more objectively and specifically. Discrimination means making a difference among objects possessing the same receptivities and existing under the same circumstances. Differentiation means making a difference among capacities that are unequal and not subject to the same circumstances.

It will be erroneous if we say that it would be better for everything in the world to be uniform and undifferentiated, for all the motion, activity and lively interchange we see in the world is made possible by differentiation.

Man has various ways of perceiving and experiencing beauty, once there is a contrast between ugliness and beauty. The attraction exerted by beauty is, in a sense, the reflection of ugliness and its power to repel.

In the same way, if man were not tested and tried in life, piety and virtue would have no value, and there would be no reason to refine one's soul and nothing from which to restrain one's desires.

If a whole canvas is covered in a uniform way, we cannot speak of it being a picture; it is the variation of color and detail that displays the skill of the artist.

In order for the identity of a thing to be known, it is essential that it be differentiated from other things, for the measure by which things or persons are recognized is the outer or inner differences they have with each other.

*****

One of the wonders of creation is the variation in the capacities and gifts with which beings are endowed. In order to ensure the continuance of social life, creation has given each individual a particular set of tastes and capacities, the interplay of which ensures the order of society; each individual meets some of the needs of society and contributes to solving some of its problems.

The natural difference of individuals with respect to capacity causes them to need each other. Everyone takes on some of the tasks of society according to his own taste and capacity, and the social life secured in that way makes it possible for man to progress and advance.

Let us take a building or an aeroplane as an example. Each of them has numerous separate parts, complex and detailed components that differ greatly from each other in size and form, this difference deriving from the responsibility that each component has toward the whole.

Were this difference not to exist in the structure of the aeroplane, it would no longer be an aeroplane but a compound of assorted metals. If differentiation is a sign of true justice in the aeroplane, it must also be an indication of divine justice among all the creatures of the world including man.

In addition, we must be aware that differentiation among beings is innate to their essence. God does not create everything with a separate and discrete exercise of His will; His will is not exercised individually. The entire world from beginning to end came into being with a single exercise of His will; it was this that enabled creatures in their infinite multiplicity to come into being.

There is, then, a specific law and order that regulates all the dimensions of creation. Within the framework of causality, it assigns a particular rank and position to everything. God's will to create and regulate the world is equivalent to His willing order in it.

There are definite philosophical proofs in support of this proposition, and it is also expounded in the Quran: *"We created everything with a certain quantity and limit; Our act is but one, like the blink of an eye."* (54:49-50)

It would be wrong to imagine that the differentiation and relations established by God in His creation are the same as the conventional relations existing in human society. God's connection with His creatures is not a mere convention or perceptual matter; it is a connection deriving from the very act of creation. The order that He has placed in all things is the result of His creating it. Every being receives from God the amount of perfection and beauty it is able to receive.

If there were no particular order regulating the world, any being might, in the course of its motions, give rise to any other being, and cause and effect might switch places. But it must be understood that the essential interrelations among things are fixed and necessary; the station and property bestowed on a thing adheres inseparably to it, whatever rank and degree of existence it may have. No phenomenon can go beyond the degree that has been fixed for it and occupy the degree of another being. Differentiation is a concomitant of the degrees of being, assigning to them differing amounts of weakness and strength, deficiency and perfection.

It would be discrimination if two phenomena had the same capacity to receive perfection but it was given only to one of them and denied to the other.

The degrees of being that exist in the order of creation cannot be compared with the conventional ranks of human society. They are real, not conventional, and not transferable. For example, men and animals cannot change places with each other in the same way that individuals can change the posts and positions they occupy in society.

The relationship connecting each cause with its effect and each effect with its cause derives from the very essences of the cause and effect respectively. If something is a cause, it is so because of some property that is inseparable from it, and if something is an effect, it is so because of a quality inherent in it, which is nothing other than the mode of its being.

There is, then, an essential and profound order that links all phenomena, and the degree of each phenomenon within the order is identical with its essence. Insofar as differentiation relates to a deficiency indwelling in the essence, it is not discrimination, because the effusion of God's bounty is not enough for a reality to come into being; the receptivity of the vessel destined to receive the bounty is also necessary. It is for this reason that certain beings suffer deprivation and do not attain higher degrees; it is impossible that a thing acquire the capacity for being or some other perfection and that God not grant it to it.

The case of numerals is exactly similar: each number has its own fixed place. Two comes after one and cannot change places with it. If we change the place of a number, we will have changed its essence at the same time.

It is clear, then, that all phenomena possess fixed ranks and modalities and are subordinate to a series of stable and immutable laws. Divine law naturally does not form a separate created entity, but an abstract concept deduced from the manner in which things are seen to exist. That which has external existence consists of the levels and degrees of being, on the one hand, and the system of cause and effect, on the other. Nothing occurs outside of this system, which is none other than the divine norm mentioned by the Quran: *"You will never find any change in the divine norm."* (35:43)

*****

The order of creation is based on a series of laws inherent in its essence. The place of every phenomenon within it is clearly defined, and the existence of the various levels and degrees of existence is a necessary consequence of the systematic nature of creation, which inevitably gives rise to variety and differentiation.

Variation and differentiation have not themselves been created; they are the inseparable attributes of all phenomena. Every particle in the universe has received whatever it had the potential to receive; no injustice or discrimination has been visited upon it, and the perfection of the universe—resembling a multiplication table in its precise and immutable ordering—has thereby been ensured.

Materialists who regard the existence of variation and differentiation in the natural order as evidence of oppression and injustice and imagine that the world is not ruled by justice will inevitably experience life as difficult, unpleasant, and wearying.

The hasty judgment of the materialist confronted by hardship and difficulty is like the verdict of a child watching a gardener pruning the healthy, green branches of a tree in the spring. Unaware of the purpose and significance of the pruning, the child will think the gardener a destructive and ignorant person.

If all the bounties of the world were placed at the disposal of the materialist, he would still not be content. For once the world is seen to be aimless and based on injustice, it is meaningless for man to seek justice, and in a world that is lacking an aim, it is absurd for man to set himself one.

If the origin and destiny of man are as the materialists depict them, such that he is a grass that grows of itself and then disappears, then man must be the most wretched of creatures. For he would be living in a world with which he lacks all affinity, compatibility and harmony. Thought, feeling and emotion would cause him distress, being nothing more than a cruel joke played on him by nature to increase his misery and wretchedness and augment his suffering.

Were a man of initiative and genius to devote himself to the service of humanity, what benefit would it hold for him? Posthumous commemorations and honorings, ceremonies held at his tomb, would not benefit him in the slightest; they would serve only to maintain a hollow legend, because the person in question would have been nothing more than a form assembled by nature for its amusement as a plaything for a few days before being turned into a handful of dust.

If we look at the fate of the majority of people who are constantly struggling with various kinds of sorrow, anxiety, deprivation and failure, the picture grows still more bleak. With such a view of human life, the only paradise materialism has to offer man is a hell of terror and pain. The materialist position that man lacks freedom and choice makes of him an even more wretched creature.

The mono-dimensional worldview of materialism would have it that man is like an automaton, with the mechanism and dynamism of its cells operated by nature. Can human intelligence and instinct—not to mention the realities of existence—accept such a banal and petty interpretation of man, his life and his destiny?

Were this interpretation to be true, man would be as incapable of experiencing happiness as a child's doll. Placed in such a situation, man would be compelled to make of his own passions and inclinations the foundation of morality and the yardstick of value, to judge all things according to personal profit and loss. He would do his utmost to destroy every obstacle in his path and loosen all restraints on his carnal desires. Were he to act otherwise, he would be regarded as backward and ignorant.

Anyone who possesses the slightest amount of insight, and judges the matter in a disinterested and dispassionate way, will regard these short-sighted and fantastic notions as valid, however much they be decked out in philosophical and scientific sophistry.

A man with a religious worldview regards the world as an orderly system possessing consciousness, will, perception and aim. The supreme justice-dispensing intelligence of God rules over the universe and every particle of being and watches over all actions and deeds. A religious man, therefore, feels a sense of responsibility vis-a-vis the consciousness that rules over the world, and knows that a world created and administered by God is necessarily a world of unity, harmony and good. He understands that contradiction and evil have an epiphenomenal existence and play a fundamental role in the achievement of good and the emergence of unity and harmony.

Furthermore, according to this worldview which sketches out broad horizons for man, life is not restricted to this world, and even the life of this world is not restricted to material well-being or freedom from effort and pain. The believer in religion will see the world as a path that must be traversed, as a place of testing, as an arena of effort. In it, the righteousness of men's deeds is tested. At the beginning of the next life, the good and the evil in the thoughts, beliefs, and actions of men will be measured in the most accurate of balances. God's justice will be revealed in its true aspect, and whatever deprivation man may have suffered in this world, whether material or otherwise, it will be made up to him.

In the light of his destiny that awaits man, and given the essential nullity of the goods of the material world, man orients his conscious striving exclusively to God. His aim becomes to live for Him and to die for Him. The vicissitudes of this world no longer claim his attention. He sees ephemeral things for what they are, and he allows nothing to seduce his heart. For he knows that the forces of seduction would cause his humanity to wither and draw him down into the whirlpool of materialistic misguidance.

*****

In conclusion, we would add that even apart from the question of receptivity, the existence of difference in the world does not imply injustice. Oppression and injustice mean that someone is subjected to discrimination although he has a claim equal to that of someone else. But beings do not have any "claim" on God nor did they ever, so if some things enjoy superiority over others this cannot count as injustice.

We have nothing of ourselves: each breath and each heartbeat, each thought and idea that passes through our mind, are taken from a stock that we do not own and have done nothing to build up. That stock is a gift from God, bestowed on us at the moment of birth.

Once we understand that whatever we have is nothing but a divine gift, it will become apparent that the differences among the gifts He gives men are based on His wisdom but have nothing to do with either justice or injustice, because there was no question of any merit or claim on our part.

This finite and temporary life is a gift to us, a present from the Creator. He has absolute discretion in deciding the type and quantity of the gift that He gives, and we have no claim upon Him.

We have, therefore, no right to object even if the gift given us quite free of charge appears slight and inconsequential.

Lesson Eighteen
A General View of the Problem

One of the questions that has always attracted the attention of thinkers concerned with the nature of human life and been the subject of eternal controversy is whether man is free to choose his aims and implement his wishes in all his deeds and activities—in all the affairs of his life, whether material or otherwise. Are his desires, inclinations and will the only factor determining his decisions?

Or are his acts and his conduct imposed upon him? Is he compelled to helplessly perform certain acts and take certain decisions? Is he an involuntary tool in the hands of factors external to himself?

In order to understand the importance of this question it must be borne in mind that on its solution depends our ability to benefit fully from economics, laws, religion, psychology and all other branches of knowledge that take man as their subject. Until we find out whether man has free will or not, whatever law be propounded for man in any of the sciences will apply to a being whose nature remains unknown to us. It is evident that no desirable result is then to be had.

The question of free will versus determinism is not exclusively an academic or philosophical problem. It is of concern, too, to all those who posit a duty for man that he is responsible for fulfilling and encourage him to do so. For if they do not, at least, implicitly believe in free will, there will be no basis for rewarding people who do their duty and punishing those who do not.

After the rise of Islam, Muslims, too, paid special attention to the question, because the worldview of Islam caused it to receive more profound scrutiny than had been the case hitherto and all the attendant obscurities to be clarified. For, on the one hand, the problem was connected with the unity of God and, on the other, with His attributes of justice and power.

Thinkers of both past and present can be divided into two categories on the question of free will vs. determinism. The first resolutely rejects the freedom of man in his actions, and if his acts appear to show the signs of free choice, this is because of the faulty and deficient nature of human perception.

The second category believes in free will and say that man enjoys complete freedom of action in the sphere of volitional acts; his ability to think and decide has far-reaching effects and is independent of all factors external to him.

Naturally, man experiences the effects of compulsion with regard to his birth, as well as various factors that surround him and occurrences he encounters during his life. The result of this may be that he ends up believing there is no such thing as free will. He entered the world involuntarily and appears to be completely controlled by fate, blown around like a piece of paper until he finally leaves the world.

At the same time, man clearly perceives that he is free and independent in many things, without any form of compulsion or imposition. He has the ability and capacity to struggle effectively against obstacles and to extend his control of nature by relying on previous experience and knowledge. An objective and practical reality he cannot deny is that there is a profound and principal difference between the volitional motions of his hands and feet and the functioning of his heart, liver and lungs.

So, given his will, awareness and ability to choose, which are a hallmark of his humanity and the source of his responsibility, man knows that he does, indeed, have free will in a whole series of acts and that no obstacle prevents him from implementing his will or forming his belief. But in other respects, his hands are tied and he has no power to choose: matters determined by material or instinctual compulsion which make up a considerable par of his life, and others that are imposed on him by factors external to him.

Determinism

The proponents of determinism do not believe that man is free in the acts he performs in the world. Theological determinists such as the Muslim theological school known as the Ash'arites, relying on the outer meaning of certain verses of the Quran and not pausing to reflect on the true meaning of all the relevant verses or on the nature of God's power to predetermine, conclude that man has no freedom whatsoever.

They also deny that things produce effects and do not acknowledge that causes have a role to play in the creation and origination of natural phenomena. They consider everything to be the direct and unmediated effect of the divine will, and they say that although man has a certain amount of will and power at his disposal, it has no effect on his acts. Men's acts are caused not by their power and their will but by God's will, which produces all effects in exclusivity. Man can only give a certain coloring to the acts he performs with his aim and intention, and this coloring results in acts being qualified as good or as bad. Apart from this, man is nothing but the locus for the implementation of God's will and power.

They also say that if we suppose man to possess free will, we will have narrowed the sphere of God's power and governance. God's absolute creativity requires that no man confront him as a creator; likewise, belief in the doctrine of the oneness of God, considering the absolute sovereignty we ascribe to Him, must mean that all created phenomena, including the acts of men, are enclosed in the sphere of the divine will and volition.

If we accept that a person creates his own acts, we deny God's sovereignty over all of creation, which is incompatible, in turn, with God's attribute of creator, for we would, then, enjoy complete sovereignty in the realm of acts and there would be no role left there for God. Thus, a belief in free will is held to lead inexorably to polytheism or dualism.

In addition, some people make the principle of determinism— whether consciously or unconsciously—an excuse for committing acts contrary to religion and morality, opening the way to all kinds of deviation in the sphere of belief and action. Certain hedonist poets belong to this group; they imagine predetermination to be sufficient excuse for their sins and hope, in this way, to escape both from the burden of conscience and from ill-repute.

*****

This determinist mode of thought is contrary to the principle of justice, with reference both to God and to human society. We clearly see divine justice manifested in all its dimensions throughout creation, and we praise His most sacred essence as possessing this attribute. The Quran says: *"God bears witness to His own oneness; He it is Who maintains justice; and His unique essence is empowered over all things and is knowledgeable of all things."* (3:18)

God also describes the establishment of justice in human society as one of the purposes for the sending of the Prophets and states this desire that His servants should maintain justice: *"Indeed We sent our messengers with proofs and miracles and sent down to them the Book and the Balance so that men should establish justice."* (57:25)

On the Day of Resurrection, God's treatment of His servants will similarly be based on justice, and no one will be subject to the slightest injustice. The Quran says: *"We will establish the scales of justice on the Day of Resurrection and none shall suffer injustice."* (21:47)

Now would it be justice to compel man to do something sinful and then to punish him for it? Were any court to issue a verdict providing for punishment under such circumstances, it would certainly be unjust.

If we deny the principle of freedom and assign no positive role at all to man's will, no difference will remain between man and the rest of creation. According to the determinists, the acts of behavior of man resemble those of other creatures in that they are caused by a series of factors beyond their control; our will does not of itself have the power to produce an effect.

But if God creates the volitional acts of man, if He is the Creator of injustice and sin, even of the assignation of partners to Himself, how can we explain such behavior on the part of a Perfect and Exalted Being?

The belief in determinism nullifies and abolishes the principles of prophethood and revelation; the concept of a divine message that is to serve as the source of human awareness; the idea of commands and prohibitions, of religious criteria and ordinances, of law and of creed; and the doctrine of certain requital for one's deeds. For once we believe that all of men's acts take place mechanically, without any will or choice on his part, no role will remain for the message of the Prophets who have been sent to assist man in his strivings.

If the duties imposed on man and the instructions addressed to him have nothing to do with his free will and ability to obey and respond, of what use are they?

If man's spiritual states and outer actions are to be mechanically determined, all the ceaseless efforts of moral educators to redeem human society and move it in the direction of creativity and higher values will be totally ineffective.

Their efforts would serve no purpose; it is fruitless to expect a being whose every act is determined to change. But man is responsible for his own salvation or destruction as well as that of others; his choice fashions his destiny, and once he knows that every act he performs has some consequence, he will choose his path with great care. His reliance on God's love and favor will cause windows of power to be opened for him.

It may be objected that considering the belief in the comprehensive knowledge of God (He has from the beginning known all that transpires in the world; nowhere in the world does an event occur, major or minor, of which He does not have prior knowledge), God must necessarily know in advance of the atrocities, evil deeds and sins men commit, and since they take place nonetheless, men are clearly unable to refrain from them.

We answer as follows. It is true that God is aware of all phenomena, both lesser and greater, but this knowledge does not mean that man is compelled in all that he does. God's knowledge is based on the principle of causality; it does not apply to phenomena or human acts that lie outside that framework. A knowledge that operates by means of cause and effect does not involve compulsion.

God was aware of the future course of events in the world and knew that men would perform certain acts in accordance with their free will. Their exercise of free will is part of the chain of causality that leads to their acts, and it is men themselves who decide to do either good or bad deeds. In the latter case, through misuse of their free will, they cause ruin and corruption, so if evil and oppression exist in a given society, this is the result of men's deeds. It is not created by God. God's knowledge has no effect on man's choice of good or evil.

It is true that within the sphere of man's freedom and power to decide, certain factors exist—such as environmental circumstances, the innate nature of man, and divine guidance—which play a role in the choices he makes. But that role is confined to the arousal of inclination, to the encouragement and assistance of man's will; it does not compel man to choose a certain direction. The existence of these factors does not mean that man is imprisoned in their grasp;

on the contrary, he is fully able either to obey the inclinations created by external factors or to resist them by confining them or changing their course. An individual can profit from the guidance available to him through insight and clear vision, giving shape to his inclinations and controlling or modifying them. The abundant instinctual drives man has within him can never be fully eliminated, but it is important to rein them in and deny them the opportunity to run wild.

*****

Suppose an expert mechanic inspects a car before it sets out on a journey and foresees that the car will not be able to proceed more than a few kilometers before stopping because of some technical defect. Now, if the car sets out and breaks down after a few kilometers, just as the mechanic has predicted, can it be said that he was the cause of the breakdown simply because he has predicted it?

Obviously not, because the car's poor state of repair was the reason for its breaking down, not the knowledge of the mechanic and the prediction he made; no rational person can regard the knowledge of the mechanic as the cause of the breakdown.

To give another example: a teacher knows of the progress his pupils are making and knows that one pupil will fail in his final examinations because of his laziness and refusal to work. Once the results of the examinations are given out, it becomes apparent that that negligent student has indeed failed to pass. Now, is the cause of such a result the knowledge of the teacher or the laziness of the pupil? Obviously, the latter.

These examples enable us to understand, to some degree, why God's knowledge is not a cause for the deeds of His servants.

*****

One of the harmful effects of determinism on society is that it makes it easier for arrogant oppressors to stifle and repress the downtrodden and more difficult for the downtrodden to defend themselves.

Using determinism as an excuse, the oppressor denies all responsibility for his violent and pitiless acts; he claims that his hand is the hand of God and attributes all his transgressions to God—God Who is beyond all reproach and objection. The oppressed are then obliged to endure and accept whatever the oppressor does with them, because to struggle against his injustice would be in vain and efforts to bring about change would inevitably fail.

The imperialists and other major criminals in history have sometimes used determinism to perpetuate their cruelty and oppression.

When the family of the Commander of the Martyrs, Husayn b. Ali, peace be upon him, came into the presence of Ibn Ziyad, that wretched criminal said to Zaynab-i-Kubra, peace be upon her: "Have you see what God did with your brother and family?"

She answered: "From God I have seen nothing but kindness and good. They have done that which God wanted of them to elevate their station and performed the duties that were entrusted to them. Soon you will all be gathered in the presence of your Lord and called to account; then you will understand who has triumphed and who has been saved."35b

In respect of the question of free will and determinism, the materialists are caught in a contradiction. On the one hand, they see man as a material being, subject, like the rest of the world, to dialectical change and unable to produce an effect of himself; faced with environmental factors, historical inevitability and pre-determined circumstances, he lacks all free will. In choosing his path of development, his ideas and acts, he is entirely at the mercy of nature. Any revolution or social development is exclusively the material result of a certain environmental situation, and man has no role to play in it.

According to the determining relationship between cause and effect, nothing occurs without its own preceding cause and man's will, too, when faced with the material and economic circumstances of his environment and mental factors, is subject to inflexible laws, being, in fact, little more than the "effect" they produce. Man is compelled to choose the path that is imposed on him by the demands of his environment and its intellectual content. There is, thus, no way for the independent will and choice of man to express itself, and no role for his sense of moral responsibility and discrimination.

But, at the same time, the materialists consider man able to influence society and the world, and they place even more emphasis than other schools of thought on propagation and ideological discipline within an organized party. They summon the masses who have been victimized by imperialism to rise up in violent revolution and try to make men change their beliefs and play a role different from that which they were previously playing—all this by relying on the power of free choice. This ascription of a role to man contradicts the whole scheme of dialectical materialism since it proclaims that free will exists after all!

If the materialists claim that arousing the oppressed masses and strengthening revolutionary movements accelerates the birth of the new order from the womb of the old, this would be illogical, because no revolution or qualitative change can take place out of turn or at other than its proper time. Nature performs its own task better than anyone, according to the dialectical method; to engage in propaganda and to seek to mobilize opinion is an unjustifiable interference in the work of nature.

It may also be said by the materialists that freedom consists in knowing the laws of nature in order to make use of them for the sake of certain goals and purposes, not in some independent stance vis-a-vis the laws of nature. But this, too, fails to solve the problem, because even after one has learned those laws and decided, in principle, to make use of them for specific purposes, the question remains of whether it is nature and matter that determine those purposes and impose them on man or man that freely chooses them.

If man is able to choose, are his decisions a reflection of the wishes and conditions of nature, or can they run counter to them?

The materialists have regarded man as a mono-dimensional creature so that even his beliefs and ideas are the result of economic and material developments and are subject to class positions and production relations within society—in short, they reflect the particular conditions arising from the material needs of human beings.

It is, of course, true that man has a material existence and that the material relations of society and physical, geographical and natural conditions all have an effect on him. But other factors, arising from within man's essential nature and his inner being, have also influenced man's destiny throughout history, and it is not possible to regard the intellectual life of man as having been inspired exclusively by matter and the relations of production. One can never overlook the important role played by religious and ideal factors, by spiritual impulses, in man's choice of a path to follow; his will is definitely one link in the causal chain leading him to do a certain act or not to do it.

No one doubts that man is subject to the influence of natural actions and reactions, and/or that the force of history and economic factors prepare the ground for the occurrence of certain events. But they are not the sole determinants of history and they do not play the fundamental role in deciding the destiny of man. They are unable to take from man his freedom and power to decide, because he has progressed to a point that he has a value which lying beyond nature enables him to acquire consciousness and a sense of responsibility.

Not only is man not a prisoner to matter and the relations of production; he has power and sovereignty over nature and the ability to change the relations of matter.

Just as changes in material phenomena are subject to external causes and factors, certain laws and norms exist in human society that determine a nation's degree of prosperity and power, or fall and decline. Historical events are neither subject to blind determinism nor accidental; they correspond to the norms and designs of creation, among which man's will holds an important place.

In numerous verses of the Glorious Quran, oppression, injustice, sin and corruption are shown to change the history of a given people, this being a norm observed in all human societies. " *When it is decided that a land shall be destroyed, the self-indulgent worshippers of profit in that society begin to work corruption and sin. Then God's ineluctable decree comes to pass concerning the vile and corrupt people who have been caught up in the deeds of pleasure-seeking hoarders of wealth: the land is turned upside down and its people are destroyed.*" (17:16)

"Did you not see what God did with the people of 'Ad? Or the people of Iram who had great power, a might the like of which had never existed in any other land? Have you not seen the people of Thamud who split the hearts of rock and raised up palaces for themselves? Or the Pharaoh who had abundant forces and troops that arrogantly wrought oppression and much corruption in the land? God brought down on them the scourge of His wrath; indeed, God lies in wait for the oppressors." (89:6-14)

The Quran also reminds us that men who worship their desires and obey their stray inclinations cause many of the calamities of history: *"Pharaoh began to act with arrogant rebelliousness in the land and cast dissension among its people, humbling and laying low the Children of Israel. He killed their sons and left alive their womenfolk; he was, indeed, given to corruption and evil."* (28:4) *"He (the Pharaoh) humbled his own people, compelling them all to obey his command; truly they were a sinful and corrupt people."* (43:54)

How much bloodshed, war, ruin and disorder has been caused by the worship of passionate desire and the hunger for power! Men, who are the component elements of society, possess intelligence and innate will in their own beings, prior to their inclusion to society; the individual spirit is not powerless vis-a-vis the collective spirit.

Those who claim that the individual is completely determined in his acts by the social environment imagine that any true compounding must necessarily involve the dissolution of the parts in the unity of the whole to enable a new reality to emerge. The only alternative to this, they believe, would be either to deny the objective reality of society as a compounding of individuals and acknowledge the independence and freedom of the individual, or to accept the reality of society as a compound and abandon the independence and freedom of the individual. It is impossible to combine these two possibilities, they maintain.

Now, although society possesses greater power than the individual, this does not mean that the individual is compelled in all his social activities and concerns. The primacy of essential nature in man—the outcome of his development on the natural plane—gives him the possibility of acting freely and rebelling against the impositions of society.

Although Islam posits personality and power for society, as well as life and death, it regards the individual as capable of resisting and struggling against corruption existing in his social environment; it does not see in class conditions determining factors leading to the emergence of uniform beliefs among those subject to them.

The duty of enjoining the good and forbidding the evil is itself a command to rebel against the orders of the social environment when these involve sin and corruption. The Quran says: *"O you who believe, hold firm to your faith, because the misguidance of others can never compel you to fall into misguidance."* (5:108) *"When they die, the angels will ask them, 'What did you do?' They will answer, 'We were weak and powerless on earth.' The angels will then say, 'Was God's earth not wide enough for you to travel in it?' (thereby escaping the environment; i.e., their excuse will not be acceptable)."* (4:97)

In this verse, those who regard themselves as compelled to conform to society are strongly condemned and their excuse for failing to assume responsibility is rejected.

For man to progress morally and spiritually, the existence of free will in him is indispensable. Man has value, and values can be expected of him, only insofar as he is free. We acquire individual independence and value only when we choose a path conforming to truth and resist the evil tendencies within ourselves and our environment by means of our own efforts. If we act only in accordance with the course of natural development or dialectical determinism, we will have lost all value and personality.

There is, then, no factor compelling man to choose a certain path in life, nor a force obliging to abandon one. Man may claim to be making himself not when he chances his form in accordance with the laws prevalent in society or pre-fashioned goals, but only when he himself chooses, decides and invests his own efforts.

Lesson Nineteen
Free Will

The proponents of this school say that man is automatically aware that he possesses freedom in his actions; he can decide as he wishes and fashion his own fate in accordance with his own will and inclinations. The existence that decrees responsibility for man, the regret man feels for certain acts he commits, the punishments the law provides for criminals, the deeds men accomplish in order to change the course of history, the foundation of science and technology—all of these prove man to be free in his actions.

Likewise, the question of man's religious accountability, the sending of the Prophets, the proclamation of divine messages, and the principle of resurrection and judgment—all these rest on man's free will and choice in the acts he performs.

It would be completely meaningless were God, on the one hand, to compel men to do certain things and, on the other, to reward or punish them. It would surely be unjust were the Creator of the world to set us on whatever path He chose, by means of His power and His will, and then to punish us for actions we have committed without any choice on our part.

If the deeds of men are, in reality, the acts of God, all corruption, evil and cruelty must be regarded as His work, whereas His most sacred being is utterly pure of all such corruption and injustice.

If there were no free choice for man, the whole concept of man's religious accountability would be unjust. The oppressive tyrant would deserve no blame and the just would merit no praise, because responsibility has meaning only within the sphere of what is possible and attainable for man.

Man deserves blame or merits praise only when he is able to decide and to act freely; otherwise, there can be no question of blame or of praise.

Those who adhere to the above position have gone to such extremes in asserting the principle of man's free will that they regard man as being the undisputed possessor of absolute free will in all his volitional acts. They imagine that God is unable to extend His rule over the will and wishes of His creatures and that men's volitional acts are excluded from the realm of His power. This, in summary, is the position of the proponents of absolute free will.

*****

Those who say that it is natural norms and the will of men that create the phenomenal world, and that neither the rotation of the world nor the acts of men have any connection with God, are ascribing all effects to a pole opposed to God. At the very least, they are making created things a partner with God in His creation, or setting up another creator in confrontation with God, the Creator. They unconsciously regard the essences of created things as independent of the divine essence.

The independence of a creature—be it man or other than man —entails belief in that creature being a partner with God in His acts and His independence, resulting clearly enough in a form of dualism. Man is, thus, led away from the lofty principle of divine unity and cast into the dangerous trap of polytheism. To accept the idea of man's absolute freedom would be to withdraw from God His sovereignty in a given area, whereas, in fact, He embraces all beings, for we would be attributing to man untrammeled and indisputable sovereignty in the sphere of his volitional acts. No true believer in God's unity can accept the existence of a creativity separate from that of God, even in the limited realm of man's acts.

While recognizing the validity of natural causes and factors, we must regard God as the true cause of all occurrences and phenomena and recognize that if God wished, He could neutralize it even in the limited sphere where it operates and render it ineffective.

Just as all creatures in the world lack independence in their essence, all being dependent on God, they also lack independence in causation and the production of effects. Hence, we have the doctrine of unity of acts, meaning perception of the fact that the entire system of being, with its causes and effects, its laws and its norms, is the work of God and comes into being from His will; every factor and cause owes to Him not only the essence of its existence, but also its ability to act and produce effects.

The unity of acts does not require us to deny the principle of cause and effect and the role that it plays in the world, or to regard everything as the direct and unmediated produce of God's will, in such a way that the existence or non-existence of causational factors would make no difference. But we should not attribute independent causation to those factors, or imagine that God's relationship to the world is like that of an artist to his work—for example, that of a painter to his painting. The work of art is dependent on the artist for its origination, but after the artist has completed his job, the charm and attractiveness of the painting remain independent of the artist; if the artist leaves this world, his brilliant work will still remain.

To imagine God's relationship with the world to be of the same type is a form of polytheism. Whoever denies the role of God in phenomena and in the deeds of men supposes, thereby, that God's power stops short at the boundaries of nature and of human free will. Such a view is rationally unacceptable, because it implies both a denial of the entirety of God's power and a limiting of that unlimited and infinite essence.

One holding such an opinion will regard himself as free of any need for God, which will cause him to rebel against Him and engage in all manner of moral corruption. By contrast, a feeling of dependence on God, of reliance on Him and submission to Him, has a positive effect on the personality, character and conduct of man. Recognizing no source of command other than God, whether inner or outer, passionate desires and inclinations will be unable to drag him this way and that, and no other man will be able to enslave him.

The Noble Quran denies man any participation with God in managing the affairs of this world: *"Say: 'Praise belongs to God alone, He Who took no offspring and Who has no partner in the managing of the world. There is never any diminution in His power that He might stand in need of a helper. Praise His essence continuously as possessing the greatest attributes of perfection.'"* (17:111)

Numerous verses unambiguously proclaim the absolute power and might of God. For example: *"God controls whatever exists in the heavens and on the earth, and He has power over all things."* (5:120) *"Nothing in the heavens or on earth can weaken God, for He is all-knowing and all-powerful."* (35:44)

The beings of this world need God for their survival and

perpetuation just as strongly as they do for their origination. The entirety of creation must receive the gift of existence anew every instant failing which the whole universe would collapse. The creativity of all the forces in the world is identical with the creativity of God and is an extension of His activity. A being that in its very essence is dependent on the divine will does not have any independent standing on its own.

Just as electric lamps derive their light from the power station which first switched on, so, too, they must constantly receive energy from the same source in order to remain alight.

The Glorious Quran emphatically and clearly declares: *"Men at all times are in need of God, and it is He alone Who is utterly free of need."* (35:15)

All essences derive from His will and are dependent on Him; all phenomena are continually sustained by Him. The powerful and magnificent order of the universe is oriented to one pole alone and turns on one axis alone.

Imam Ja'far as-Sadiq, upon whom be peace, said: "The power and might of God are too lofty for aught to occur in the universe that is contrary to His will."[36]

Had God not bestowed on us the principle of free will and were He not every instant to endow us with life, resources and energy, we would never be able to do anything. For it is His unchanging will that has determined that we should perform volitional acts according to free will, thereby fulfilling the role He has assigned to us. He has willed that man should construct his own future, good or bad, bright or dark, in accordance with his own discernment and desires.

Our volitional acts are, then, connected both with ourselves and with God. We can use the resources God has placed at our disposal in full awareness either to uplift and improve ourselves in accordance with a correct choice, or to plunge into corruption, sin and self-indulgence. It remains, of course, true that the scope of our volitional acts lies within a fixed framework; power is from God, and the use made of it, from us.

Suppose that someone has an artificial heart, powered by a battery that we can switch on and off in a control room; whenever we want, we can turn off the switch and stop the heart functioning. That which lies within our power is the current that goes from the battery to the heart; at any moment we can stop it. But as long as we allow the battery to function, the person in which the heart is implanted will be free to act as he wishes. If he performs a good or an evil act, it will, without doubt, be in accordance with his own will. The way in which he makes use of the power we have placed at his disposal depends entirely on him and has nothing to do with us.

Similarly, our power derives from God and He can withdraw it from us at any moment, but He has assigned the manner in which we make use of that power entirely to our free choice.

The Median School

All beings in the world enjoy a form of guidance particular to the stage of development they have reached; their specific forms of guidance correspond to their different degrees of existence.

It is possible for us to clarify and distinguish our own position among the different beings in this world. We know that plants are captives in the hands of the determining forces of nature, while exhibiting, at the same time, certain slight developmental reactions vis-a-vis changes in their environment.

When we analyze the properties of animals, we feel that they possess attributes quite different from those of the plants. In order to obtain their nourishment, animals have to engage in a wide range of activities, since nature does not invite them to a feast at which their nutritional needs are placed before them. Animals need certain tools and instruments in their efforts to gain food, and these nature has provided them with.

Although animals are subject to the strong pull of the instincts and are, in this sense, subjugated beings, they enjoy a certain degree of freedom by means of which they can free themselves, to some extent, from the harsh captivity of nature.

Scientists are of the opinion that the weaker animals are with their respect to their natural structure and organs, the stronger they are with respect to their instincts and the more they enjoy the direct aid and protection of nature. Conversely, the better equipped they are as regards sensory and conceptual powers and the greater their degree of independence, the lesser the extent to which they are guided by instinct. In the first period of his life, the child is covered directly by the comprehensive protection of his father and mother;

as he grows, he gradually emerges from their all-encompassing supervision.

Man who has attained the highest level of development as the only being possessing the faculty of independent will and discernment, has a relatively low level of instinctual power. As he gradually attains his freedom, he is progressively beset with relative weakness in his sensory capacities.

Nature satisfies in various ways all the different needs of the plants. In the animal realm, although the mother has to make certain efforts to carry, nurture and protect her offspring, instincts appear very early in the young and the mother need not concern herself with training and educating them. But in the case of man, we see that he does not possess powerful natural instincts, and his power to resist unfavorable and hostile environmental factors is much inferior to that of the animals. Thus, his dependence on his parents continues for many years until he finally attains independence and self-sufficiency and is able to stand on his own feet.

*****

The Noble Quran speaks clearly of man's weakness and impotence: *"Man was created weak and impotent."* (4:28) Nature has left man to his own devices far more than the animals. We see in man, on the one hand, an unfolding of freedom and an emergence of a capacity to grow and gain awareness, and, on the other, an increase in dependence and neediness. While enjoying a relative freedom, man is powerfully drawn deeper and deeper into the thralls of need.

These varying situations of different orders of creation constitute, in the view of certain thinkers, factors impelling growth and development. The farther a being advances on the ladder of progress, the closer it comes toward freedom. It is precisely neediness and lack of innate equilibrium that enable growth and advancement to take place.

For free will and choice to express themselves, a factor opposing natural instinct must exist. Man will, then, be caught between two opposing attractions, each seeking to gain his obedience, so that he is compelled to choose the path he desires, freely, consciously, and relying on his own efforts and resources. Free of all determining factors and mental preconceptions, he begins the work of making and developing himself on the basis of specific principles and criteria.

Once faced with this element of contradiction, man cannot attain equilibrium or choose a correct path for himself by acting as an automaton or refraining from all effort. Bearing as he does the burden of the divine trust, the great divine gift that the heavens and the earth were unfit to receive, man alone proving worthy of accepting it, man is confronted with only two choices in his conflict and struggle. Either he becomes a prisoner to the tyranny of instinct and unbridled desire, thus debasing and degrading himself; or, drawing on his abundant capacities of will, thought and decision, he embarks on the path of growth and development and begins to ascend.

*****

Whenever a being is freed from compulsory obedience to the instincts, casts off the chains of servitude, and beings to make use both of its innate capacities and its acquired abilities, its sensory faculties are weakened and its natural capacities diminish.

The reason for this is that any organ or capacity left stagnant and unused in a living being gradually stultifies. Conversely, the more intensively an organ or capacity is used, the more it will grow and be filled with energy.

So, when the light of man's conscious and creative will, inspired by the power of discernment and reason, lights his path and determines his actions, his power of insight and thought enable him to discover new truths and realities.

Furthermore, man's state of bewilderment and hesitation between two opposing poles inclines him to reflect and assess, so that through rational exertion he can distinguish the right path from the wrong. This will activate his mental faculties, strengthen his reflective capacities, and endow him with a greater degree of motion and vitality.

Ownership, the desire for liberty, science and civilization—all these are the direct result of man's exercise of his free will. Once man attains freedom and continues his necessary and positive efforts, eh can advance swiftly in the processes of growth and the unfolding of all aspects of his innate, essential nature. As his talents and capacities mature, he will be transformed into a source of benefit and virtue in society.

We see the results of free will everywhere, and the struggle waged against its proponents by those who oppose it is itself a clear indication that the latter implicitly accept it.

Now let us see what limits are set on man's power of choice and what scope he enjoys in the exercise of this faculty.

The authentic view of Shi'ism, which is drawn from the Quran and the words of the Imams, represents a third school, intermediate between the determinists and the proponents of absolute free will. This school does not suffer from the inadequacies and weaknesses of determinism, which contradicts reason, conscience and all ethical and social criteria and denies God's justice by attributing to Him all the atrocities and injustices that take place, nor by asserting absolute free will does it deny the universality of God's power and reject the oneness of God's acts.

It is obvious that our volitional acts differ from the motions of the sun, the moon and the earth, or the movements of plants and animals. Will power arises from within us and makes it possible for us to perform or not to perform a certain deed, thus giving us freedom of choice.

Our ability to choose freely whether to perform good or evil deeds arises from our freely exercised capacity of discernment. We must use our gift of free choice consciously; first, we must reflect maturely and carefully, weigh things with precision, and then make a calculated choice. It is God's will that we should use our freedom in this way in the world that He has created, with consciousness and alertness.

Whatever we do is definitely included in the sphere of God's antecedent knowledge and will. All aspects of life, all that touches on the destiny of man, is limited by and conditional on His knowledge; it is defined by limits already existing in God's knowledge. Furthermore, we are not free of need for a single instant of that Essence to which we are connected, and the use of the powers inherent in our being is impossible without God's continuous aid.

With His supreme, overwhelming power, He closely watches us, and in a way beyond our imagination, He has complete awareness and sovereignty over all our intentions and deeds.

Finally, our free will cannot go beyond the limits of the order established by God in this creation, and it does not, therefore, create any problem with respect to the oneness of God's acts.

While being able to create effects in the world by means of his will, man is, himself, subject to a series of natural laws. He enters the world without any choice on his part, and closes his eyes on the world without any desire to do so. Nature has fettered him with instincts and needs. Nonetheless, man possesses certain capacities and abilities; freedom produces a creativity within him which enables him to subjugate nature and establish dominance over his environment.

Imam Ja'far Sadiq, peace be upon him, said: "Neither determinism nor free will; the truth of the matter lies between these two."[37]

So there is free will, but it is not all-embracing, because to posit a separate sphere for man would be equivalent to assigning God a partner in His acts. The free will that man enjoys is willed by the Creator of nature, and God's command manifests itself in the form of the norms that rule man and nature, natural relations, causes, and factors.

*****

In the view of Islam, man is neither a ready-made creature, condemned to determination by fate, nor has he been cast forth into a dark and purposeless environment. He is a being overflowing with aspirations, talents, skills, creative awareness and diverse inclinations, accompanied by a kind of indwelling guidance.

The mistake made both by the determinists and the protagonists of unlimited free will is that they have imagined man to have only two possible roads before him: either all his acts must be attributed exclusively to God, so that he then loses all freedom and becomes determined in his acts, or we are obliged to accept that his volitional acts derive from an independent and unbounded essence, a view entailing the limitation of God's power.

However, the fact that we have free will does not affect the comprehensiveness of God's power, because He has willed that we should freely take our own decisions, in accordance with the norm and law He has established.

From one point of view, man's acts and deeds can be attributed to him, and from another point of view, to God. Man has a direct, immediate relationship with his own deeds, while God's relationship with those deeds is indirect, but both forms of relationship are real and true. Neither does human will set itself up in opposition to the divine will, nor is man's will contrary to what God desires.

Obstinate men intent on disbelief, who oppose all kind of preaching and warning, initially take up their erroneous position though an exercise of free will, and then experience the consequences of their obstinacy and blindness of heart, visited on them by God.

Obeying the desires of their lower self, these people of inequity prevent their hearts, their eyes and ears from functioning, and, as a result, earn a state of eternal perdition.

The Quran says: *"Whether you warn them or warn them not, they will not believe you. God has placed a seal on their hearts; there is a veil over their ears and their eyes, and a painful torment awaits them."* (2:6-7)

Sometimes corruption and sin are not of such magnitude that they block the path of return to God and the truth. But at other times they reach an extent that the return to true human identity is no longer possible; then the seal of obstinacy is set on the polluted spirits of the unbelievers. This is an entirely natural result of their behavior, determined by God's will and desire.

The accountability of such persons originates in their exercise of free will, and the fact that they have not acquired the blessings of guidance does not lessen their accountability. There is a firm and self-evident principle to the effect that "whatever originates in free will and culminates in compulsion does not contradict free will."

The Imam is related to have said: "God wished that things should take place through causes and means, and He decreed nothing except by means of a cause; He, therefore, created a cause for all things."[38]

One of the causes employed by God in His creation is man and his will, in keeping with the principle that particular causes and means are established by God for the appearance of every phenomenon in the universe: the occurrence of the phenomenon necessitates the prior existence of those causes and means, and were it not for them, the phenomenon would not appear.

This is a universal principle which inevitably governs our volitional actions as well. Our choice and free will come to form the last link in a chain of causes and means that result in the performance of an act on our part.

The Quranic verses which relate all things to God and depict them as arising from Him are concerned with proclaiming the pre-eternal will of the Creator as the designer of the world and explaining how His power embraces and penetrates the entire course of being. His power extends through every part of the universe, with no exceptions, but God's unchallenged might does not diminish the freedom of man. For it is God Who makes free will a part of man, and it is He Who bestows it upon him. He has made man free to follow the path of his own choosing, and He holds no individual or people accountable for the failings of another.

If there is any compulsion in the affairs of man, it is only in the sense that he is compelled to have free will, as a consequence of God's will, not in the sense that he is condemned to act in a given way.

So when we undertake the best of deeds, the capacity to perform them is from God, and the choice to use that capacity is from us.

Certain other verses of the Quran clearly emphasize the role of man's will and actions, decisively refuting the views of the determinists. When it wishes to draw man's attention to the calamities and torments he endures in this world, it describes them as being the result of his misdeeds.

In all the verses that are concerned with God's will, not even one can be found which attributes man's volitional acts to the divine will. Thus, the Quran proclaims: *"Whoever does the smallest good deed shall experience the result of it, and whoever does the slightest evil deed shall experience the result of it."* (99:7-8) *"Certainly you are accountable for what you do."* (16:93) *"Those who assign partners to God say that their worship of idols and other deeds derive from God's will; had God not willed it, they and their forefathers would not have become polytheists, and they would not practice the deeds of the Age of Ignorance. Those who went astray in previous times also spoke such nonsense, denying the heavenly teachings and attributing their misguidance to God but they suffered the punishment for their lies and their slander. Say to them, O Prophet: 'Do you have a decisive proof for what you say? If you do not, your excuses are nothing but the result of erroneous ideas and fantasies; you speak vainly and lyingly.' "* (6:148)

Were the salvation and misguidance of man to be dependent on God's will, no trace of misguidance or corruption would exist upon earth; all would follow the path of salvation and truth whether they wished to or not.

Certain miscreants who seek excuses for themselves have

claimed that whatever sinful acts they commit are willed and desired by God. Thus the Quran says: *"When they commit some abominable act, they say: 'We found our forefathers doing this, and God has commanded us to do it.' Tell them, O Prophet, 'God never commands men to commit foul deeds, but you attribute to God every sinful and erroneous act you commit in your ignorance.' "* (7:28)

In just the same way that God has willed a reward for good acts, so, too, He has willed punishment for sin and corruption, but in both cases, willing the result is different from willing the act that leads to the result.

Man's being and the natural effects of his acts are, indeed, subject to God's will, but his volitional acts arise from his own will.

The view of Islam, as conceived by Shi'ism, is that man does not possess such absolute free will that he is able to act outside the framework of God's will and desire, which cover the entire universe in the forms of fixed laws and norms, thus reducing God to a weak and impotent entity when confronted with the will of His own creatures. At the same time, man is also not prisoner to a mechanism that prevents him from choosing his own path in life and compels him, like the animals, to be a slave to his instincts.

The Noble Quran clearly states in some of its verses that God has shown man the path to salvation, but he is compelled neither to accept guidance and salvation nor to fall into misguidance.

"We have shown man the path of truth and the path of falsehood; he may choose either the path of guidance and offer the thanks, or choose the path of ingratitude." (76:3)

To attribute man's volitional acts to God is, therefore, rejected by the Quran.

Lesson Twenty
The Forms of God's Will and Volition

Fate and destiny are one of those controversial topics that are often misinterpreted because of lack of precise understanding or, sometimes, malicious intention. In order to explore the topic, we will analyze it here as concisely as possible.

Everything in this world is based on a precise calculation, logic and law. It has been put in its place according to an exact measurement, and it derives its defining characteristics from the causes and factors on which it is dependent.

Just as every phenomenon derives its primal existence from its specific cause, it also acquires all its outer and inner properties from the same source; it derives its shape and extent from the cause. Since there is a homogeneity between the cause and the effect, the cause inevitably transmits to the effect a characteristic bearing affinity to its own essence.

In the worldview of Islam, fate and destiny have the meaning of God's firm decree concerning the unfolding of the affairs of the world, their extent and their limits. All phenomena that occur within the order of creation, including man's deeds, become fixed and certain by means of their causes, their being a consequence of the universal validity of the principle of causality.

Fate (*qada'*) has the meaning of something terminated and irreversible, and it refers to the creativity and the acts of God. Destiny (*qadar*) has the meaning of extent or proportion and it indicates the nature and quality of the order of creation, its systematic character; it means that God has endowed the world of being with a planned and systematic structure. In other words, destiny is the result of His creativity as it leaves its impress on all created things.

To express it differently, what is meant by destiny is the external and objective fixing of the limits and proportions of a thing, externally and objectively, not mentally. Before executing his plan, an architect will prepare in his mind the qualities and dimensions of the complex he proposes to build. The Quran speaks of these fixed forms, properties and proportions of things as *qadar*: *"We have created everything according to a fixed proportion."* (54:49) *"God has fixed a quantity and proportion for all things."* (65:3)

The term, fate (*qada'*), in the Quran means rational and natural necessities, all the parts of the cause that lead to the emergence of a thing. It implies that God's will will implement itself only when the fixed quantities, conditions and causes of a thing are aligned with each other.

The Creator takes into consideration the spatio-temporal situation of all phenomena, together with their limits and proportions, and then issues His decree based on them. Whatever factor or cause is visible in the world is the manifestation of God's will and knowledge and the instrument for the fulfillment of what He has fated.

*****

The capacity for growth and development is fixed in the very heart of things. Matter, which is subject to the law of motion, has the capacity of assuming different forms and traversing various processes. Under the influence of different factors, it assumes a whole variety of states and qualities. It derives energy from certain natural factors that enable it to advance, but when it encounters certain other factors, it loses its existence and vanishes. Sometimes it continues to advance through different stages until it approaches the highest degree of development; at other times, it lacks the necessary speed to advance through further stages of progress and moves sluggishly.

So, the outcome of things is not directly connected with fate and destiny because it is the cause that determines the nature of the effect. Since material beings are connected with a variety of causes, they will necessarily follow different paths; each cause fixes the being subordinate to it in a particular path.

Imagine that someone is suffering from appendicitis. This is a "destiny" arising from a particular cause. Two additional, separate "destinies" await this invalid: either he agrees to surgery, in which case he will recover his health, or he fails to agree, in which case he dies. Both of these choices represent a form of destiny.

Destinies can, then, be interchangeable, but whatever decision the invalid takes and acts upon will not be outside the sphere of what God has destined.

One cannot sit with hands folded and tell oneself, "If it is my fate, I will remain alive, and if it is not my fate, I will die, whatever efforts I make to be treated."

If you seek treatment and recover, this is your destiny, and if you refuse treatment and die, that, too, is your destiny. Wherever you go and whatever you do, you are in the embrace of destiny.

People who are lazy and refuse to work first decide not to work and then when they are penniless, they throw the blame on destiny. If they had decided to work, the money they earned would equally have been the result of destiny. Thus, whether you are active and diligent or idle, you in no way contravene destiny.

A change in destiny does not, then, mean the rebellion of a certain factor against fate or opposition to the law of causality. No factor producing an effect in the world can be exempt from the universal law of causality. Something that causes a change in destiny is, itself, one link in the chain of causality, one manifestation of fate and destiny. To put it differently, one destiny is changed by means of another destiny.

In contrast with the sciences that point in only one direction and show the orientation only of certain aspects of phenomena, the laws of metaphysics are not concerned with phenomena from the conjunctural point of view although the laws do regulate the phenomena, they are indifferent with respect to the orientation they assume. In reality, both the phenomena themselves and their orientation are subject to the vast and comprehensive laws of metaphysics: in whatever direction the phenomena tend, they are still held inescapably in the embrace of those laws.

The situation is like that of an expansive, broad plain; even its most northerly and most southerly parts are included within the plain.

*****

In short, fate and destiny represent nothing other than the universality of the principle of causality; they represent a metaphysical truth that cannot be measured in the same way as the data of science.

The principle of causality says only that every phenomenon

has a cause; it cannot of itself make any prediction, this being a property totally absent from metaphysical awareness.

For the laws of metaphysics, which is a descriptive form of knowledge and the firm and stable ground for the various phenomena of the world, it makes no difference which particular phenomena occur. A highway along which men travel thanks to its firmness and stability is completely indifferent to the direction in which they are travelling.

Ali, peace be upon him, the Commander of the Faithful, was resting in the shade of a broken wall that seemed likely to collapse. Suddenly he arose and went to sit in the shade of another wall. He was asked: "Are you fleeing what God has destined?"

He said, "I am taking refuge in God's power from what He has destined," meaning, "I am fleeing from one destiny to another destiny. Both siting and rising were equally subject to destiny. If the broken wall collapses on me and I am harmed, it will be fate and destiny, and if I leave the zone of danger and escape all harm, that, too, will be fate and destiny."

The Glorious Quran describes as divine norms the systems and laws of nature that rule over the world and follow inevitable and immutable courses: *"The divine norm is immutable and unchanging."* (33:62)

The immutable norm of God decrees, among other things, that: *"If a people provides itself with the capital of faith and performs good and worthy deeds, it will be triumphant on the stage of life and win the viceregency of the earth."* (24:55)

According to the Quran, this, too, is an immutable divine norm: *"God will never change the destiny of a society until its people change that society."* (13:11)

From the point of view of the religious worldview, realities are not confined within the four walls of material causation. Phenomena ought not to be considered purely in their sensory relations and their material dimensions. Non-material factors have access to realms that are totally closed off to material factors, and they have an independent and decisive role in the emergence of phenomena.

The world is by no means indifferent to the distinction between good and bad; man's acts produce certain reactions during his lifetime. Kindness and benevolence toward one's fellows and the love and service of God's creatures are factors that, through non-material means, ultimately result in a change of human destiny and contribute to tranquility, happiness, and an abundance of blessings.

Oppression, malevolence, egoism, aggression also bear bitter fruit and have inevitably harmful results. So, from this point of view, some form of requital is inherent in nature, for the world possesses perception and consciousness; it sees and it hears. The manner in which it requites deeds is one manifestation of fate and destiny; it is impossible to flee from it, for wherever you go, it will seize you.

A certain scientist says: "Do not say the world lacks perception, for you will then have accused yourself of lacking perception. You have come into being as part of the world, and if there is no awareness in the world, there is none in you either."

Concerning the role of non-material factors in fashioning destiny, the Quran says the following: *"Were the people of the earth to believe and act with piety, We would open to them the gates of all heavenly and earthly blessings, but since they denied the truth, We punished them for their evil behavior."* (7:96) *"We never destroy a region unless its people become cruel and aggressive."* (28:59)

The concepts of fate and destiny are cited by the proponents of determinism as one of their proofs. In their opinion, it is not possible for any act to be performed independently by anyone, for God has predestined the acts of man, general and particular, good and bad, so that no scope remains for any volitional acts on his part.

There is a difference between determinism and irreversible destiny. Every phenomenon is bound to occur once all of its causes are present. One link in the chain of causes is man's will, which plays a definite role of its own. Man is a being endowed with free will, hence his acts pursue definite goals, and in pursuit of those goals, he does not follow some automatic law of nature, like raindrops that fall in accordance with the law of gravity. Were it to be otherwise, man could not, in fact, pursue the goals he has in mind as a being possessing free will.

This is in contrast with the determinist view, which regards the free will of man as inoperative and relates all causes exclusively to God and to factors external to man's own essence.

Belief in fate and destiny results in determinism only when they are regarded as supplanting man's powers and will, so that no role or effect is ascribed to his wishes in the acts he performs. In reality, however, fate and destiny are nothing other than the system of cause and effect.

The Quran proclaims that some of those who opposed the Prophets and raised the banner of rebellion against the chosen of God interpreted fate and destiny in a determinist sense. They did not want the existing situation to change in such a way that the social order of monotheism should replace the rotten customs to which they were attached.

These are the relevant verses: *"They said, 'If God wanted us not to worship the angels, we would not do so.' They speak not in accordance with logic or scientific proof, but with their own vain imaginings. Did We ever send them a book containing proofs for their erroneous belief in determinism?"* (43:20-21)

By contrast with the determinists, the messengers of God and the followers of heavenly teachings have been concerned not with the preservation of the status quo but with the overthrow of traditions and looking toward the future.

The Noble Quran promises mankind ultimate victory in its struggle against tyrants and emphasizes that the final government to rule upon the earth will be the government of justice; falsehood will vanish and the final outcome of all affairs will belong to the Godfearing. This is the promise of the Quran: *"It is Our will that We show favor to those who have been oppressed throughout history by making them leaders and the inheritors of the earth."* (28:5) *"God promises those among you who believe and do good deeds that He will make you viceregents on earth, that He will firmly establish the religion He has chosen for you, and that He will bestow on all the believers safety after their fear of the enemy——this, in order that you might worship Me alone and not ascribe to Me any partners."* (24:55)

"We made the people who had been oppressed to inherit the blessed and promised land. Thus did the favor of God to the Children of Israel reach its full measure, and as a reward for their patience in enduring hardship We destroyed Pharaoh and his people together with all they had wrought." (7:137)

So the Quran depicts an opposition between belief and unbelief, between the deprived and the tyrannical, and it tells us that the world is moving toward the triumph of truth over falsehood, of the deprived over their oppressors; a revolutionary movement is underway that is in harmony with the motion of all creation toward perfection.

The call of the Prophets, reward and punishment, paradise and hellfire—all these prove that man has duties and responsibilities, and the Quran accordingly links man's salvation in this world and the hereafter to his deeds.

According to the doctrine of fate and destiny, man is free and responsible for his own destiny and in control of it. Fate and destiny are, indeed, at work if one people is powerful and another, wretched and humble, if one community is triumphant and proud, and another, defeated and humble. This is only because fate and destiny determine that one people make use of the means of progress and advancement and walk on the path of honor and dignity, while another chooses self-indulgence and indifference, and can expect nothing but defeat, humiliation and wretchedness.

The Quran clearly states: *"God never changes the state of a people until they themselves change their own situation."* (8:53) No doubt it may happen that our wishes are not fulfilled as we expect, but this does not in any way prove that man is compelled and determined in his acts. The fact that the scope of man's volitional acts is limited does not in any way contradict his definite possession of free will; to assert that man has free will in no way implies that his free will is unlimited.

God has set numerous factors to work throughout the vast expanse of being. Sometimes these factors, together with the phenomena in which they result, are evident to man, and sometimes they are not. A careful and realistic interpretation of the concept of fate and destiny will inspire man to strive harder to know and to recognize all of those factors, so that by taking them into account, he can aspire to still greater accomplishments.

It is precisely because of the limitations of man's capacities that he is unable to acquire all the factors needed for success so that his wishes and desires remain unfulfilled.

In accordance with the general principle of causality, the destiny of every being is tied to the causes that precede it. Whether one accepts the existence of a divine principle or not has no bearing on the question of the freedom and destiny of man, because one may either attribute the system of cause and effect to the will of God, or assume that it is independent and has no connection to a divine principle. This being the case, it can also not be maintained that determinism results from belief in the doctrine of fate and destiny. What we mean by destiny is the inseparable link of every phenomenon with its causes, including the will and choice of man; we are certainly not denying causality.

Fate and destiny bring forth the existence of every phenomenon by means of its particular cause. The divine will rules over the entire world as a universal principle and law. Any change that takes place is also on the basis of a divine custom or norm. Were this not to be the case, fate and destiny would never have any external expression. Any scientific school of thought that accepts the principle of universal causality is obliged to accept the reality of the relations between a phenomenon and its cause, whether it is theistic or materialistic in its outlook.

Now, if a definite link between the occurrence of a phenomenon—including human acts—and its causes leads to man being an automaton, predetermined in his acts, both theism and materialism are open to objection, insofar as they both accept causality. But if it does not lead to that conclusion (as indeed it should not), the question still arises: what is the difference, in this respect, between theism and materialism?

*****

The difference is that the theistic worldview, in contrast with that of materialism, regards ideal and non-material factors as fully capable of exerting an effect. Those factors are, indeed, more subtle and complex in the web of creation than are material factors. The worldview based on belief in God gives spirit, aim and meaning to life. It bestows on man courage, vitality, breadth of vision, profundity of insight, and strength of mind; prevents him from falling into the abyss of purposelessness; and bears him upward in an unending arc of ascent.

So, a believer in God who is firmly convinced of fate and destiny, who perceives that there are wise purposes at work in the creation of man and the universe, will advance on the straight path through his reliance on God; knowing himself to be supported and protected by God, he will be more confident and hopeful of the results of his activity.

But one who is caught up in the worldview of materialism, whose mental framework inclines him to belief in a material fate and destiny, enjoys none of these advantages. He is deprived of a sure and invincible support in striving to attain his goals.

It is, then, obvious that there is a profound difference between the two schools of thought as far as their social and psychological effects are concerned. Anatole France says: "It is the beneficial effect of religion that teaches man the reason for his existence and the consequence of his deeds. Once we reject the principles of theistic philosophy, as almost all of now do in this age of science and freedom, we no longer have any means of knowing why we came into this world and what we are meant to accomplish after setting foot in this world.

"The mystery of destiny has enveloped us with its powerful secrets, and if we wish completely to avoid experiencing the sorrowful ambiguity of life, we must not think at all. For the root of our sorrow lies in our complete ignorance of the reason for our existence. Physical and spiritual pain, torment of the soul and the senses—all would be bearable if we knew the reason for them and believed God to have willed them.

"The true believer takes pleasure in the spiritual torment he endures. Even the sins he commits do not rob him of hope. But in a world where the ray of faith has been extinguished, pain and sickness lose their meaning and become ugly jokes, a form of sinister ridicule."

Lesson Twenty-one
An Improper Interpretation
of Fate and Destiny

Some pseudo-intellectuals have erroneous ideas about fate and destiny and imagine that this doctrine causes stagnation and inactivity, restraining man from all forms of effort to improve his life.

The source of this notion in the West is a lack of adequate understanding of the concept, particularly as it is expounded in Islamic teachings. In the East, it has gained influence because of decline and backwardness.

It is fairly well-known that whenever individuals or historical communities fail to reach its goals and ideals, for whatever reason, they console themselves with words such as "luck," "accident," "destiny," "fate."

The Most Noble Messenger, peace and blessings be upon him, expressed himself eloquently on this matter: "An age will come for the people of my community when they will commit sin and inequity, and in order to justify their corruption and pollution, they will say: 'God's fate and destiny decreed that we act thus.' If you encounter such people, tell them I disown them."

Belief in fate and destiny does not prevent man from striving to reach his goals in life. As those who have the necessary religious knowledge realize, Islam calls on human beings to strive to the utmost in improving their lives, both morally and materially. This is, in itself, a powerful factor in intensifying the efforts man makes.

One of the Western thinkers who has an inadequate understanding of fate and destiny is Jean-Paul Sartre. He imagines it is impossible simultaneously to believe in a fate and destiny determined by God and in the freedom of man, and that it is, therefore, necessary to choose either belief in God or the freedom of man: "Because I believe in freedom, I cannot believe in God, because if I believe in God, I will have to accept the concept of fate, and if I accept fate, I will have to renounce freedom. Since I am attached to freedom, I do not believe in God."

However, there is no contradiction between belief in fate, on the one hand, and the freedom of man, on the other. While regarding God's will to be universal in scope, the Noble Quran also ascribes a free and active role to man, describing him as capable of consciously fashioning his own destiny with a knowledge of good and bad, ugly and beautiful, and the capacity to choose between them. *"We have shown the path to man, and he is free to choose the right path and be thankful or to choose the path of ingratitude."* (76:3) *"Whoever wishes for the eternal abode and strives for it as needed will find his efforts rewarded."* (17:19)

Those who on the Day of Judgment seek refuge in determinism and say: *"If God wished, we would not worship other than Him,"* (16:35) are rebuked for attributing their own sinfulness and error to divine will and fate.

In none of the verses of the Quran are the corrupt and evil deeds of individuals or societies attributed to fate and destiny. Equally, fate and destiny are not depicted as obstacles to a corrupt and polluted society's reforming itself. Not a single verse can be found in which God's will has supplanted man's will, or in which it is said that men started to suffer because of fate and destiny.

The Quran repeatedly mentions the wrath of God that will overtake the tyrannical and corrupt, bringing painful punishment in its wake.

Since God is extremely loving and merciful to His servants, having bestowed countless bounties on them, and is, at the same time, clement and ready to accept repentance, He always keeps open for the sinner the path of return to purity and rectitude. God's acceptance of repentance is, in itself, a great instance of His mercy.

Although the scope of man's will is greater and more extensive than that of all other known living creatures and plays a more creative role, his will has effect only in areas delimited for his activity and deeds by God. He cannot, therefore, accomplish everything he wants throughout his life.

It often happens that man decides to do something but however hard he tries, he is unable to accomplish it. The reason for this is not that God's will opposes itself to man's will and prevents him from doing what he wishes. It is rather that in such cases some unknown external factor which lies beyond the scope of man's knowledge and control creates obstacles in his way and prevents him from attaining his goals.

Both individuals and societies constantly encounter such obstacles. Considering the fact that in the natural realm there is no cause without an effect and no effect without a cause, and that our means of perception are limited to this world and to the human realm, it should not be difficult for us to accept that our aspirations may not be fulfilled as we desire.

God has set billions of factors to work in the order of being. Sometimes those factors are apparent to man, at other times they remain unknown to him and cannot be incorporated in his calculations. This, too, relates to fate and destiny, but not only does it not result in depriving man of free will or prevent him from striving to attain satisfaction in life; it also guides him in both thought and activity and imbues the very depths of his being with greater vitality. He seeks to augment his knowledge and identify, as precisely as possible, the factors that pave the way for attaining greater success in life. Belief in fate and destiny is then a potent factor in advancing man toward his aims and ideals.

*****

The question of the salvation or damnation of man is implicitly solved in the preceding discussion, since salvation and damnation arise from the deeds and acts of men, not from matters that lie beyond their will or from natural phenomena that have been implanted in human existence by the Creator.

Neither environmental and hereditary factors nor the natural capacities present in man have any effect on man's salvation or damnation; they cannot fashion his destiny. That which fixes man's future, is the axis on which his salvation or damnation turns and the cause of his ascent or descent, is the degree to which man, as a being endowed with choice, makes proper use of his intellect and knowledge and other powers.

Happiness and salvation do not depend on an abundance of natural capacities. It is, however, true that the one who has greater capacities than others also bears greater responsibilities. A slight error on his part is far more significant than a similar error on the part of a weak and powerless individual. Everyone will be called to account in accordance with the talents and capacities he possesses.

It is entirely possible that a person whose innate capacities and resources are slight should order his life in accordance with the duties and responsibilities that have been imposed on him and reach that true happiness which alone is worthy of the lofty station of man. What will enable him to achieve that result is the intensity of his efforts he expends in order to make correct use of the limited capacities he has been given.

Conversely, one who has been given abundant inward resources and capacities, not only may not use them to benefit himself, he may actually misuse them to trample on his own human dignity; and cast himself into the swamp of corruption and sin. Such a person is, without a doubt, a sinner destined to damnation and will never catch a glimpse of salvation.

The Quran says: *"Every soul will be held in pledge for what it has acquired."* (74:38) Hence, the salvation or damnation of a person is dependent on the volitional acts, not on his natural or psychological make-up. This is the clearest manifestation of God's justice.

*****

One of the characteristic doctrines of Shi'ism is *bida'*, a term meaning that men's destinies change when the factors and causes regulating them change: what appears to be eternal and immutable changes in accordance with a change in man's conduct and acts. Just as material factors can reshape a man's destiny, non-material factors may also elicit new phenomena.

It is possible that such non-material factors may make apparent what is hidden and contrary to the apparent course of affairs. In fact, through a change in causes and circumstances, God will decree that a new phenomenon will appear, more beneficial than the phenomenon it has replaced. This is comparable to the principle of abrogation in revealed law. If an earlier law is abrogated in favor of another, this does not indicate ignorance or regret on the part of the divine lawgiver, but only that the validity of the abrogated law has expired.

We cannot interpret the concept of *bida'* in the sense of God changing His mind after the reality of something previously unknown to him becomes known to Him. This would contradict the principle of the universality of God's knowledge and so it cannot be accepted by any Muslim.

*****

Petitionary prayer is another factor, the effectiveness of which should not be belittled. It is obvious that God is aware of the inner-most secrets of everyone, but in man's relationship with God, petitionary prayer plays the same role as man's efforts and acts in his relationship with nature. Quite apart from its psychological effect, prayer exercises an independent effect.

Every instant new phenomena appear in nature in the emer-gence of which preceding causes play a role. Likewise, in one great sphere of existence, petitionary prayer is profoundly effective in advancing man toward his goals. In just the same way that God has assigned a role in the system of causality to each of the natural elements, so, too, He has assigned an important role to petitionary prayer.

When a person is besieged by difficulties, he must not fall into hopelessness and despair. The doors of God's mercy are never closed to anyone. It may be that tomorrow a new situation emerges in no wise corresponding to what he had anticipated. For, as the Quran says: *"Each day God is engaged in a different affair."* (55:29)

One should, therefore, never relinquish one's efforts. A peti-tionary prayer that is not joined to appropriate efforts is, as the Mas-ter of the Godfearing, Ali, peace be upon him, has said, "Like a person who wishes to loose an arrow from a bow without a string."

While making continuous efforts, one should place one's de-sires before God, in hope and sincerity, and seek aid with one's whole being from that source of infinite power. God will then certainly take one by the hand and aid him. The Quran says: *"When My servants ask you whether I am far from them, distant or near, let them know that I am near to them. Whoever calls upon Me, I shall answer him and fulfill his prayer. Let them hearken to My call and believe in Me in order to attain happiness."* (2:186)

Man's spirit will ascend toward God and immerse him in true happiness when he avoids the pitfall of neediness by severing himself from all causes and turning directly to God. He will then see himself linked directly to God's essence and palpably feel His infinite favor and grace.

Imam Sajjad, peace be upon him, addresses God as follows in the prayer known as the Prayer of Abu Hamza: "O Creator! I see the paths of request and petition leading to You open and smooth and the sources of hope in You abundant. I see it permissible to request aid from Your favor and mercy, and I see the gates of prayer open to all who call upon You and beg for Your aid. I am certain that You are prepared to answer the prayer of those who call upon You and to grant refuge to those who seek it with You."38a

There is also a tradition concerning the effects of sin and good deeds: "Those who die on account of sin are more numerous than those who die on account of natural death, and those who live on account of performing good deeds are more numerous than those who live on account of their natural life span."39

It was the effect of prayer that enabled Zakariya, a true Prophet who had despaired of having a child, to attain his desire; it was the effect of repentance that saved the Prophet Yunus and his people from disaster and annihilation.

The laws that the great Creator has implanted in the system of the universe do not in any way limit His infinite power or lessen its scope. He has the same absolute discretion in changing those laws, in confirming or abrogating their effects, as He did in establishing them. That Unique Essence, Whose careful and comprehensive supervision covers the whole system of being, can hardly be helplessly subject to laws and phenomena He Himself has created, or lose the power and capacity to do whatsoever He wills.

When we say that God is able at any instant to change the phenomena He has created in the world, we do not mean that He destroys the order of the world and its fixed regulations or overturns the laws and principles of nature. The very process of change takes place in accordance with certain unknown principles and criteria that escape our limited perception and cognition. If man looks carefully and critically at the matter and takes into consideration the wide range of possibilities with which he is confronted, it will prevent him from ambitiously attempting to predict all things on the basis of those few principles which he has been able to observe in the natural realm.

Endnotes

1. Russell, *Why I am not a Christian.*, p. 37.
2. King, *Sociology*, p. 99.
3. *Du'a-yi 'Arafa* in *Mafatih al-Janan*, p. 265..
4. *Bihar al-Anwar*, III, p. 41.
5. *Nahj al-Balaghah.*, ed. Subhi Salih, p. 43.
6. There is a clear reference to this matter in the following words of Imam Sajjad, upon whom be peace: "Pure and exalted are You, O Lord, Who knows the weight of the heavens! Pure and exalted are You, O Lord, Who knows the weight of the earth! Pure and exalted are You, O Lord, Who knows the weight of the darkness and the light! Pure and exalted are You, O Lord, Who knows the weight of the shade and air!" (*Sahifa-yi Saniya*, prayer 55).
6a. *Hiss-i-Dini*, translated by Engineer Bayani.
7. *Bihar al-Anwar*, III, pp. 51-53.
8. *Tafssir al-Mizan*, Vol. VIII, p. 255.
9. *Bihar al-Anwar*, III, pp. 103-104.
10. Morrison, *Raz-i Afarinish*, pp. 102-104.
11. *Bihar al-Anwar*, II, p. 21.
12. Russell, *Why I am not a Christian*, p. 9.
13. Quoted in Furughi, *Sayr-i Hikmat dar Urupa*, III, p. 162.
14. Will Durant, *History of Philosophy*, II, p. 497.
15. Russel, *Why I am not a Christian*, p. 20.
16. *Bihar al-Anwar*, I, p. 166.
17. *Isbat-i Vujud-i Khuda*, p. 17.
18. This is reminiscent of the Quranic verse that says, *"If all the trees in the world were to be turned into pens, and the seven seas together with an additional ocean were turned into ink, the recording of God's words would still be incomplete, for truly God possesses wisdom and power."* (18:109)
19. *Dau Hazar Danishman dar Justuju-yi Khuda-yi Buzurg*, p. 13.
20. *Isbat-i Vujud-i Khuda*, p. 60.
20a. *Bihar al-Anwar*, Vol. III, p. 152.
21. Shaykh al-Mufid, *Irshad*, p. 142.
22. *Mafatih al-Janan.*, p. 400.

23. *Nahj al-Balaghah*, Sermon 220.

24. *Nahj al-Balaghah*, Sermon 225.

25. *Sahifa-yi Sajjadiya*, pp. 163-198.

26. *Dau Hazar Danishmand dar Justuju-yi Khuda-yi Buzurg*, pp. 61 and 99.

27. *Nahj al-Balaghah*, Sermon 181.

28. *Nahj al-Balaghah*, ed. Fayz al-Islam, p. 14.

29. *Usul al-Kafi, Kitab at-Tauhid*, p. 150.

30. *Usul al-Kafi, Kitab at-Tauhid*.

31. *Nahj al-Balaghah*, Sermon 159.

32. *Bihar al-Anwar*, IV, p. 143.

33. Saduq, *Tauhid*, p. 73.

34. *Bihar al-Anwar*, III, p. 297.

35. *Kifayat al-Muwahhidin*, I, p. 442.

35a. *Nahj al-Balaghah*, ed., Subhi Salh, p. 493.

35b. *Muntaha al-Amal*, p. 299.

36. *al-Kafi*, I, p. 160.

37. *al-Kafi*, I, p. 160.

38. *al-Kafi*, I, p. 183.

38a. *Mafatih al-Janan*, p. 185.

39. *Safinat al-Bihar*, I, p. 488.

General Index

Publications of the Islamic Education Center

Du'a-yeh-Kumail with Persian translation
Du'a-yeh-Kumail with Urdu translation
Du'a-yeh-Kumail with English translation
The Holy Quran with Persian translation
A Shi'ite Creed by Shaykh as-Saduq in Persian